T0098137

Practical Kung Fu Street Defense

100 Ways to Stop an Attacker in Five Moves or Less

Waysun Johnny Tsai

TRIUMPH
BOOKS

Copyright © 2008 by Waysun Johnny Tsai

No part of this publication may be reproduced, stored in a retrieval system, or transmitted in any form by any means, electronic, mechanical, photocopying, or otherwise, without the prior written permission of the publisher, Triumph Books, 542 South Dearborn Street, Suite 750, Chicago, Illinois 60605.

Triumph Books and colophon are registered trademarks of Random House, Inc.

Library of Congress Cataloging-in-Publication Data

Tsai, Waysun Johnny.
  Practical kung fu street defense : 100 ways to stop an attacker in five moves or less / Waysun Johnny Tsai.
      p. cm.
  Includes bibliographical references and index.
  ISBN-13: 978-1-60078-082-0 (alk. paper)
  ISBN-10: 1-60078-082-2 (alk. paper)
  1. Kung fu. 2. Martial arts weapons. I. Title.
  GV1114.7.T73 2008
  796.815'9--dc22

                                                          2008012683

This book is available in quantity at special discounts for your group or organization. For further information, contact:

Triumph Books
542 South Dearborn Street
Suite 750
Chicago, Illinois 60605
(312) 939-3330
Fax (312) 663-3557

Printed in U.S.A.
ISBN: 978-1-60078-082-0
Design by Patricia Frey
Photos on pages vi–x courtesy of Carl Nolan Thurman. Photos on pages 1–272 courtesy of Oren Headen. Cover photo courtesy of John Talley.

This book is dedicated to the innovators of progressive martial arts and anyone who is willing to take the time to learn how to stand and defend their loved ones (and him- or herself) against the immediate danger of an attacker.

"Without students, there would be no teachers."
—Waysun Johnny Tsai

Contents

Grandmaster Tom Saviano, Grandmaster Steven G. Abbate, UFC Veteran Keith Hackney, and Waysun Johnny Tsai in 2005.

Foreword

Practical Kung Fu: 100 ways to stop an attacker in five moves or less. *Wow.* What a statement.

As a black belt practitioner in more than five different systems of martial arts, I am able to look at these techniques and know that they are traditional. As a former four-time bare knuckle UFC veteran, and MMA veteran Hall of Fame coach of the year, I know they are effective and valuable to any person as a form of self defense, whether experienced or novice. There are palm strikes in here that are identical to the palm strike I used to knock down a 6'8" 616-pound sumo wrestler in UFC who was three times my size.

As an MMA pro fighter and seasoned street fighter, I recommend these hand-to-hand combat techniques. With the instruction and step-by-step photos offered in this book, it makes it easy for anyone currently interested in defending his- or herself in all types of situations. These techniques are beyond excellent and useful in everyday situations; they may save your life one day.

Demonstrated on these pages are a hundred different combinations that are designed to be similar enough that they can blend together and create a never-ending "flow" of techniques. This book is all about practical fighting at its best; with a hundred different scenarios there is something here for everyone to walk away with—young, old, experienced, or beginner. I am confident you will enjoy Waysun Johnny Tsai's *Practical Kung Fu Street Defense.*

—Keith Hackney

Congressman Jesse Jackson Jr. training with Waysun
Johnny Tsai.

Foreword

When my Kung Fu master, Waysun Johnny Tsai, told me that he was releasing a book on his martial arts methodology, I got excited. I thought, *finally—a book where a Shaolin Kung Fu expert shows the "practical side of Shaolin Kung Fu."*

I have been a private student of Master Waysun Johnny Tsai for several years now, and I have to say, his martial arts skills are both beautiful and deadly effective.

I am a lifelong fan and practitioner of the arts. I hold a black belt in Tae Kwon Do and karate, and I like to box. I also hold a first degree black sash under Master Waysun Johnny Tsai. Practicing Shaolin Chuan Fa with him over the years helped me connect the dots on all my martial arts training to create a better flow from technique to technique—my moves adapting and evolving, always growing from within with each lesson. His teachings break down the basic fundamentals of fighting arts and make them effective, fast, and powerful.

Practical Kung Fu Street Defense is a perfect introduction to his perspectives and techniques for real life.

This book reminds us of how important, effective, and easy it is to learn the basics. In here,

Master Waysun doesn't teach or demonstrate the fancy, beautiful Kung Fu that we see in film (no flipping animal style, no acrobatic jumping, or wushu butterfly kicks are to be found in these pages). Instead you will find a hundred different, yet similar, combinations and responses to a wide variety of very realistic and common attacks.

You will find combinations that make the inexperienced say, "That's it? That's all? I can do that!" That's exactly what Master Waysun wants to teach: easy, effective self-defense. At the same time, the book offers more than enough martial arts substance for an experienced or expert practitioner to appreciate and learn some moves.

Knee kicks, throat shots, knees to the face, and eye gouges are all included. That's what this book is about—the ugly, practical side of Kung Fu fighting.

As I stated earlier, I am excited about this book. I finally have something from my Sifu that I can keep at my side during my travels to use for practice!

Enjoy!

—Jesse Jackson Jr., Illinois Congressman

Waysun Johnny Tsai with students.

Introduction

Kung Fu. When you read it, when you hear it, when you see it, what do you think of? Bruce Lee releasing the ferociousness of his one-inch punch, Jackie Chan taking out 20 guys in a movie set street fight, Jet Li flipping over two attackers while he finishes one off in midair. Whether it's cartoon characters or hip-hop videos, Kung Fu has become a major influence on mainstream culture. Its explosive power and rapid-fire techniques have more to offer than entertainment.

What about the stuff that's underneath it all? This book brings you face-to-face with the core of what Kung Fu is: a practical, down and dirty, effective means for street self-defense.

Practical Kung Fu Street Defense is written for the beginner, the street fighter, the experienced martial artist, and the curious alike. It is packed full of information that will help you understand the fight and stop the attacker.

This book strips away the flowery movements of Kung Fu and takes it down to the bare essentials. You will understand why a martial artist trains the way he or she does. *Practical Kung Fu Street Defense* shows you step-by-step how to take the stuff you find on the training floor and use it for realistic, hand-to-hand combat and real-life situations.

You will learn to recognize and control combat ranges. Why care about stance work and angles? Find out here. How do you read your opponent's telegraph? Learn it here. You will develop stun, crippling, and knockout shots. Develop defenses against sneak attacks, ground fighting, and multiple assailants. The techniques in this book are focused on one goal and one goal only: to stop and drop an attacker as fast and furiously as possible.

Make no mistake, this is not a book about the self-defense techniques of a true system, but a book of fresh perspectives that a martial arts enthusiast of any level or the average "guy on the street" can use and should keep within an arm's reach. *Practical Kung Fu Street Defense* is a book about application without tags and true no-holds-barred fighting.

These techniques have been taught to and used by thousands of people across the country, ranging from soccer moms and busy executives to police officers, FBI agents, and members of congress. They have previously been presented via the seminar circuit from the United States to Brazil. Now *Practical Kung Fu Street Defense* can be read and studied on the commute to work, on a business or leisure flight, or the comforts of your own home.

Chapter 1

The Basics

The only way Kung Fu can work on a practical level is by developing a few simple fundamental strengths that assist in everything you do. We have all heard the catchphrases—a solid house must have a strong foundation; the sturdiest oak has the deepest roots. Nowhere does this apply more than in the ability to defend yourself effectively.

We will present three fundamental principles in this chapter: stance work, angles, and combat ranges. Once you develop an understanding of what these three areas cover and how to apply them during an attack, it will be easy to put them together for some simple and effective practical street defense.

Stance Work

Remember your schoolyard days back when you were a child? At least once, there was someone attempting to push you or hit you in some fashion. What did you do? Stand there and let them?

Move, move, move! There is never any reason to stand in the line of an attack.

Once you have moved, you are in a good position to take advantage of your opponent's vulnerability. He has just spent himself releasing the first attack. He is surprised there was nothing for his attack to land on. Use these seconds of surprise to your advantage.

You've created a window of opportunity, and it is time to strike. You must counter with enough force to stun and disable your attacker. Who wants to duke it out? Maximum blocking and striking power comes from the ability of your legs to generate enough power from the ground and through your body.

Stance work builds the ability to root yourself and uproot your attacker. It develops the capability of moving out of the way properly or positioning yourself properly for a counterattack. It is the first step in learning how to use the entire body for maximum blocking and striking power.

"Rooting" means dropping your center so it is not simple to pick you up or knock you off your feet. "Uprooting" is getting underneath your attacker and disrupting his or her center with little effort. It means knocking an opponent off balance.

Make no mistake, stance work is important and there is no shortcut around it. If you are serious about taking the techniques presented here and learning how to use them, don't skip this chapter.

The Traditional Kung Fu Horse Stance

Feet are shoulder-width apart or slightly wider. Knees are bent and directly over your ankles. Your feet should be straight, toes pointed forward. Most of your weight should be to the center or back of your foot. Ideally, thighs are parallel to the floor. Spine is straight. (Figure 1–1a)

Figure 1-1a

Figure 1-1b

Do this correctly for one minute and see how your legs feel. If you have trouble maintaining the correct alignment, hold the position against the wall. (Figure 1–1b)

What It Develops

The traditional Kung Fu Horse Stance builds strength in the legs. It develops hip flexibility and lower-leg flexibility. It instructs the body on where proper anatomical alignment is. You learn where your center is and what it means to have 50 percent of your weight on either leg.

How to Use It

The Horse Stance is used to root against side attacks. Stand in a relaxed position and have a friend push you from the side. (Figure 1–1c) What happens?

Start again and drop your center into a more traditional Horse Stance. Have your friend push you again. (Figure 1–1d) Any difference?

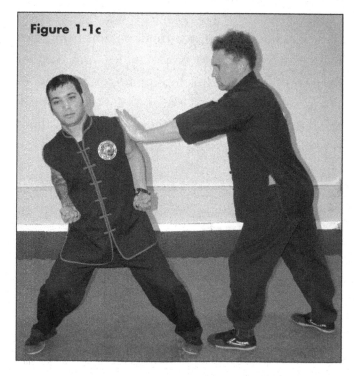

Figure 1-1c

Experiment with dropping into the Horse Stance so that it comes more naturally. (Figure 1–1e)

The Horse Stance is also used to root against grabs. Stand in a relaxed position and have another friend grab you from behind in a bear hug. Use a different friend since the first one is exhausted from all that pushing. See if friend number two can lift you. (Figure 1–1f)

Have your friend grab you again. This time drop down into a traditional Horse Stance. (Figure 1–1g)

Figure 1-1f

Figure 1-1d

Figure 1-1e

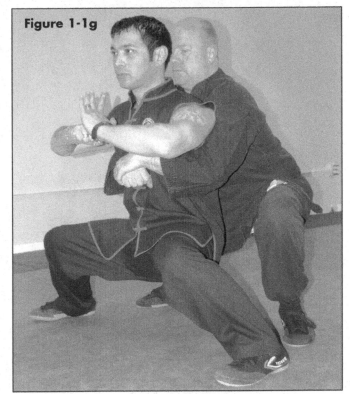

Figure 1-1g

Any easier to lift you? No? That's the magic of the Horse Stance.

What? It's still easy to lift you? Then have your friend grab you again. Drop down and hook a foot behind his leg. (Figure 1–1h)

The Traditional Kung Fu Bow and Arrow Stance

Stand with your feet wider than shoulder-width, with your heels lined up. Rotate the toes of both feet 45° to the right. Bend your right leg, make sure your knee is over your ankle and your thigh is parallel to the floor. Your left leg should be locked with the hip rotated toward the floor. Seventy percent of your body weight should be on the front leg, 30 percent on the back. (Figures 1–2a–b) Do the opposite to work the other side.

Figure 1-1h

What It Develops

The traditional Kung Fu Bow and Arrow Stance builds strength in the legs. It develops hip and leg flexibility. It helps you learn how to project forward momentum while keeping your center. It teaches you how to thrust off of the back leg.

How to Use It

The Bow and Arrow Stance builds a root against forward attacks. By working the bow, you acquire the ability to spring off your back leg and get out of the range of an attack. You also can drive in to

Figure 1-2a

Figure 1-2b

your opponent's range to counter. It develops proper weight shifting for maximum blocking and striking power.

Remember what we said about moving? We never want to get in the way of a forward attack—ever. But we are not all Jackie Chan and sometimes it happens. The Bow and Arrow Stance helps you learn to absorb a blow without getting knocked off your feet.

To get a sense of what we are talking about, get into a traditional Bow and Arrow Stance. Have an adult in your family or a trusted friend stand in

front of you. Make sure you are in a good stance with the back leg locked. Have your family member push at your shoulders and try to move you off your feet. (Figures 1–2c–d)

Getting hit gets old very fast. So let's use the Bow and Arrow Stance to get out the way instead. Have someone in your family or a trusted friend stand in front of you and then step on a straight line with one hand out. His or her hand should be pointed to the middle of your chest. (Figure 1–2e)

Your job is to stand in front of him or her and extend your arms, in line with your shoulders, 45° to the corners. (Figure 1–2f) The direction of your arms is the direction you are going to use to get out of the way. Stepping with one leg to an out

Figure 1-2c

Figure 1-2d

Figure 1-2e

Figure 1-2f

side and shifting to your bow stance, remove yourself from the line of attack. (Figure 1–2g)

You've made it and got out of the way without incident. Now you can decide if you want to block or counter.

Go back to the starting position. This time put your hands out in front of you in a loose position. Have your partner step in again. Step to the right angle again and turn and shift your body to the left, putting your weight on the left leg as you shift. Your hands should make contact with your partner's arm as you shift your weight. (Figures 1–2h–j)

Congratulations! You have accomplished Kung Fu Street Defense Rule #1—*move!* On top of that, you have just learned Kung Fu Street Defense Rule #2—*block!*

The Traditional Kung Fu Cat Stance

Stand with your feet wider than shoulder-width, with your heels lined up. Rotate the toes of both feet 45° to the right. Shift most of your weight to your left. Bend your left leg, make sure your knee is over your ankle and your thigh is almost parallel to the floor. Bend your right leg, and lift your

Figure 1-2h

Figure 1-2i

Figure 1-2g

Figure 1-2j

right heel so that the ball of your right foot is on the floor. Weight distribution for the Cat Stance is 90° on the left leg and 10° on your right. Your back should be straight. (Figures 1–3a–b)

Do the opposite to work the other side.

What It Develops

The traditional Kung Fu Cat Stance builds strength in the legs. It develops hip flexibility. It helps you learn how to load one leg while keeping your center. It develops thrusting power off of the back leg. It helps you understand the balance and weight shift for moving out of the way and using an effective kick as a counter.

How to Use It

The Cat Stance helps you root effectively on one leg. It continues to expand upon the *move* concept of getting out of the way. It is not as dynamic as the step with the Bow and Arrow, but there is a reason. Just as the cat is a sneakier animal, you develop the subtlety of turning your waist to deflect a blow. You rotate your centerline out of the way and with the line of the attack.

The Cat Stance also frees the other leg for proper weight distribution to kick with maximum blocking and striking power.

Have your partner stand in front of you again and step straight in. It is important that he or she steps straight in. Step to the left side and sink onto your leg left into the traditional Cat Stance. Notice the center of your body turns toward the outstretched arm? (Figures 1–3c–e)

Here is another drill, but work it slowly at first and pick up speed as you get comfortable. Have your partner step in again and allow him or her to touch your chest. The minute you feel the slightest bit of touch, step into the Cat Stance and turn your waist. By working this and working it faster as

Figure 1-3a

Figure 1-3b

Figure 1-3c

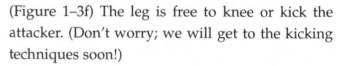

Figure 1-3d

you get comfortable, you learn to get out of the way quickly and at the most appropriate moment. You don't want to show your hand too soon and allow the attacker to adjust.

Time for another round. Have your partner step in again with his or her arm outstretched and again attempting to touch you. Step out of the way into the Cat Stance and lift your leg slightly.

(Figure 1–3f) The leg is free to knee or kick the attacker. (Don't worry; we will get to the kicking techniques soon!)

If you are off balance, you are leaning as you step and turn. More practice will prevent this from happening, but if you just can't get the step, we've got that covered, too.

Practice these until they feel more natural.

Figure 1-3e

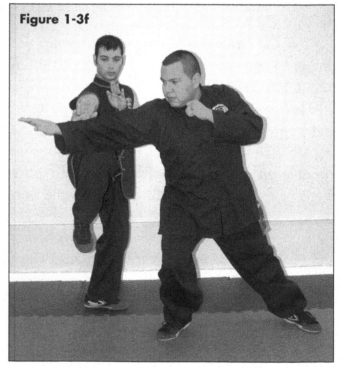

Figure 1-3f

In the next two stances, we are leaving out the word "traditional." Traditional stances are exercises that build the body in specific ways. Now we are moving onto natural body positions from the get-go. In reality, no one would ever defend himself or herself from a traditional stance. The ability to adapt and move quickly are key components to defending yourself effectively.

Use the traditional stances as exercises to develop the body for self-defense. They teach the nervous system what to do when you have to respond.

The Passive Defensive Stance

Stand with your feet shoulder-width apart. Your legs should be slightly bent. Place your hands in front of you. One hand should extend a little farther than the other. Palms are facing out and slightly down and fingers are relaxed but together. (Figures 1–4a–b)

This stance helps to protect your personal space.

How to Use It

We all have a sense of what our personal space is. Stay in one piece by making sure no one enters that personal space. The second you get a sense someone intends to break your personal zone, the hands go up to protect your centerline. Distribute your weight evenly. Stand up straight and make good eye contact.

It is quicker for your hands to find a target from this position. They are already halfway there. You are in a position of strength, but are not exciting the attacker any more or less than he already is. (Figures 1–4c–d)

Figure 1-4a

Figure 1-4b

Figure 1-4c

Figure 1-4d

The Fighting Cat Stance

Stand with your feet in line with your shoulders, one foot forward and one foot back. Your center should be in the middle of both feet. Sink 80–90 percent of your weight onto your back leg. Your hands should be stretched out in front of your chest, one hand slightly forward from the other. (Figures 1–5a–b) Your hands should be held in fists or with fingers together and thumbs tucked in. (Figures 1–5c–d)

How to Use It

The Fighting Cat Stance is a ready position from which you can step or root as discussed with the traditional stances.

You can root from this stance by evening your legs and centering your weight. You can spring to an angle to avoid a straight-line attack and shift back in to counter. You can step to the side to root and turn the centerline.

Have two or three friends take turns coming in at different angles. Remember Kung Fu Street Defense Rule #1—move. Once you're out of the way, work on turning in toward your attacker in order to counter.

Angles

We've covered this already and you didn't even realize it. See, Kung Fu is easy!

Imagine you're standing in the center of a square. There are eight directions you can move.

Working the angles refers to where you want to go to get out of the way. We all tend to move forward or backward as a first instinct. By itself there is nothing wrong with that. It just isn't the safest direction to move.

Working angles also refers to where your opponent will be most vulnerable. Once you move, it is best to find yourself in the safest spot

Figure 1-5a

Figure 1-5c

Figure 1-5b

Figure 1-5d

for you and the most vulnerable spot for your adversary. When an attacker comes in on a straight line, moving on an angle gives you the advantage. The angle put you in an "open" area on your opponent or in his blind spot. Countering from this area will be the most effective. You can then escape or end the attack.

Horse Stance	Side-to-side attacks
Bow and Arrow Stance	Left upper corner/ side-to-side
	Right upper corner/ side-to-side
Cat Stance	Left rear corner/upper right corner counter

Combat Ranges

Combat ranges represent your distance from the attacker at any given moment during the conflict. The combat range you find yourself in will determine how you respond to an adversary. A prior knowledge and understanding of these ranges will give you a distinct advantage in overcoming your opponent.

Combat Range #1: Long to Intermediate Distance

You and your opponent are far enough away from each other that even extending a leg completely would not make contact with him. (Figure 1–6a) This is the longest distance in Combat Range #1.

If one of you steps in with a kick and gets close enough to strike with an extended punch, you have entered the intermediate distance of Combat Range #1. You each have entered each other's personal zones. You are making contact with each other, but are not right on top of each other.

What It Means

Defensively, Combat Range #1 allows you to bob and weave. It is easier to stay out of harm's way since you have room to move before the opponent makes contact.

Offensively, you can attack with the fists or feet using longer punches and kicks at full extension of the leg. It offers you the ability to hit or kick and have a real possibility of moving out of range safely and quickly.

Combat Range #2: Short Distance

You are no longer at the end of your opponent's extended limbs. You are at the attacker's "inside." Shorter striking techniques work in this range— tight hook punches, uppercuts, or an elbow or knee. (Figure 1–6b)

What It Means

Defensively, Combat Range #2 requires that you cover your vital areas more diligently. It is a better place to be if someone is using a long weapon against you (such as a bat), because it cuts off the length and is easier for you to jam.

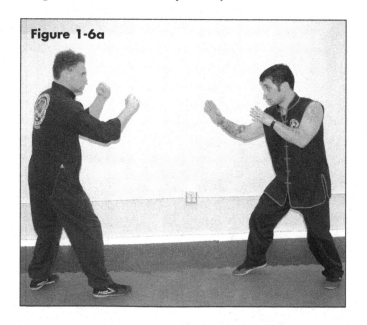

Figure 1-6a

Offensively, you have put the attacker in the same sort of situation. You are closer to all the vital striking areas—eyes, nose, throat, solar plexus, and groin. Once you strike it is harder to get out of this range, so it is imperative to strike with accuracy and intent.

Combat Range #3: No Distance

You are literally right on top of each other, but not on the ground. What's called "grappling" starts to happen in this range. Joint manipulation, grabs and holds, sweeps and throws occur in this range. (Figure 1–6c)

What It Means

Defensively, choking is the biggest problem in this range. Once oxygen is cut off to the brain, you will obviously be incapable of defending yourself any further. Being swept or thrown is another common defensive problem. Once you are thrown to the ground, you have to get up to your feet first in order to escape. You are at greater risk of being pinned. These situations are not impossible to get out of, but the more immobile you are the fewer options you have.

Offensively, the disadvantages listed become your advantages. What gives you the edge in this situation? A better root, a better sense of your center, a better understanding of attack angles—more practice at developing these aspects gives you the advantage in such close-quarter combat.

Combat Range #4: Ground Fighting

You are on top of each other *and* on the ground using joint manipulation, grabs, and holds. (Figure 1–6d)

Figure 1-6b

Figure 1-6c

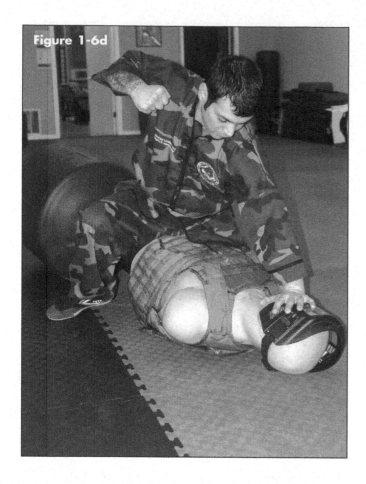

Figure 1-6d

What It Means

Defensively, positioning yourself for good leverage is key to getting out of a pin. You must be aware that body weight will play a significant factor in this range. The heavier opponent has a distinct advantage.

Offensively, you must have good knowledge of body mechanics and the range of motion of the limbs of the body. You must understand how to use your body weight effectively. You must be aware of where your center is and where your attacker's center is while in a prone position. This range represents the thinking man's fight.

Although you may see a lot of MMA fights on television like the UFC, remember those fighters are still in a very controlled environment and it is a sport with plenty of rules and a referee to break the fight when things go too far. In real combative situations, there are no rule or referees, so if you hit the ground, your ultimate goal is to get back up to your feet as soon as possible. Grappling for arm bars and submissions in a street fight will tie up your hands and possibly get you kicked and stomped in the face by your attacker's buddies.

Training for grappling is an essential part of becoming a complete fighter, and it is highly recommended. While training, courage comes in packs, and if you are unfortunate enough to get jumped, don't sacrifice your 60 percent of your arsenal and tackle one of your attackers, tying up your limbs. If you are taken down, do your best to fight your way back to your feet; you have a better chance if you're standing. Also, trying to use range 4 against a knife attack is a bad idea. While ranges 2 and 3 will work better, please keep in mind the first defense against a knife should always be distance and getting away. There is always a great chance of getting cut in a knife fight.

In Summary

You have started developing the means to execute practical Kung Fu street defense. Stance work is how you take the clay—your physical body—and start shaping it into the ultimate self-defense tool. By applying your knowledge of angles and combat ranges you can use this tool in the most efficient manner possible.

Read on to discover how to determine what your attacker will do, even before he or she makes a move!

Chapter 2

The Telegraph

The "telegraph" is the movement, twitch, or expression created *before* a fighter attacks. All combatants telegraph to some extent. The very best professional fighters have learned to eliminate or minimize their telegraphs. They have learned to read the telegraph of their opponents. The talent to do this sets the extraordinary fighter apart from the mediocre one.

All martial arts, along with Kung Fu, are a form of self-expression. This self-expression has its place if you're an actor in action flicks. It has its place if you are a form or kata competitor in the local or national tournament circuit. But make no mistake about it—tense faces, screaming kicks, and jumping into a "movie-type Kung Fu master stance" will ultimately work against you.

Stealth and surprise are powerful allies when it comes to combat.

For our purposes, the ability to read and minimize the telegraph can mean succumbing to an attack or finding yourself in one piece and able to go on with your life. Understand that this skill is that important.

We will present two fundamental principles about the telegraph in this chapter: how to read it and how to minimize it. Learning how doesn't only apply to a knockdown, drag-out fight. Learning to do this can prevent an event from happening. It can stop the event in a matter of seconds if it does start.

Once you develop an understanding of the telegraph, it will be easy to apply what you know to all kinds of situations and use this knowledge for simple, effective, practical street defense.

Reading the Telegraph

Reading an attacker's telegraph takes practice and patience. Like any skill, the more you do it, the better at it you will become.

With that being said, there are some simple body movements you can look for when a potential threat is facing you. These simple body movements will alert you on how and when they will strike.

Body Tension and Facial Expression

Where does the intention to strike start? It starts in the mind, of course. Once the desire to hit or kick is in the mind, the next reflective response is a slight tension that builds in the muscles of the body and the expression on the face.

Body tension will show up in a lifting of the shoulder, a cocking of the arm, and a flinch of the torso. It is almost as if the body is winding up to release its energy now that the commitment to strike is there.

We all know how to read facial expressions. Reading expressions is something we learn as infants as we try to determine the moods of our parents.

For combat, we are refining what we already know how to do. We are looking for a grimace along the eyebrows, a widening of the eyes, or a pursing of the lips. Just as all people smile when they are happy, all people have similar facial tics right before they strike. (Figure 2–1a)

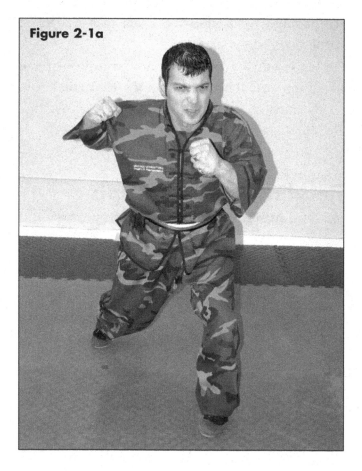

Figure 2-1a

How to Practice
You-on-You

First, practice on your own to see the kind of expression you make before you strike. Stand in front of a mirror in the Fighting Cat Stance with your right shoulder pointed toward the mirror.

Throw a couple of jabs with intention and study what happens to your body and face before you strike. The more you can bring up the feeling of really trying to hit somebody, the better you will be able to understand the telegraph. In other words, throw it like you mean it!

Try another technique like the back fist and see what happens. Does your fist clench, jaw line tighten, and elbow move? Now throw a kick and see what happens to your shoulder and torso.

Now stand square in the mirror with your centerline facing you in Passive Defensive Stance. Keep your hands down at your sides and throw a spear hand from this position. Put your hands in front of you to protect your centerline and throw the spear hand again. Notice any differences in how your body moves? Notice any similarities?

One-on-One

Now grab a partner and practice in front of each other. Have one person work at being the attacker while the other just observes. Make sure you are a safe enough distance away from each other so that you don't actually hit each other. Look for similarities to your own telegraphs you saw when you were working in the mirror. Look for differences.

Switch roles.

Once you feel you can both read each other fairly well, start stepping or sliding in with your attacks. What kind of difference does this make? Do the telegraphs become more gross or subtle?

How to Use It

With the appropriate amount of practice, your reflexes will start to develop, sharpen, and react appropriately and efficiently. As your reflexes and senses develop, your autonomic nervous system will react faster than your conscious mind. You will find yourself responding to movement directed at you within your personal safety zone without having to think too much about it.

The more you practice this by yourself and with different partners, the better your automatic response will become.

Minimizing Your Own Telegraph

If reading a "tell" in your adversary gives you an advantage, the next logical thought is that minimizing any telegraphic movement of your own gives you an even greater edge.

This means making an effort to minimize any movement in yourself that can alert your opponent to the fact that you are about to strike. Minimizing these movements, like anything else in effective street self-defense, takes practice.

Why bother practicing this very important skill? Telegraphing your move to an attacker is like screaming, "Here comes my right hook to your face…stop it if you can!" Exposing the technique and skill you possess will give the attacker the upper hand in defending against it.

Be smart. Slip that shot in before he knows what hit him. That's the best way to "take someone out," when they are least expecting it and are not bracing for some sort of impact.

How to Practice
You-on-You

You have already practiced in front of a mirror to see the kind of expression you make before you strike. Go back in front of the mirror and stand in the Fighting Cat Stance with your right shoulder pointed toward the mirror.

This time your goal is to strike while keeping a poker face.

Throw a couple of jabs and keep your face nondescript. Now smile and see if you can throw a few while keeping the same smile on your face. Smile before, during, and after you strike. The more you can hide the intention of really trying to hit somebody, the better you will be able to hide your technique.

Try another technique like the back fist. This time see if you can throw it while you are talking. Concentrate on relaxing your shoulders and body. Don't stare at the area you intend to hit. Be sneaky and deceptive, yet effective and absolute.

Now stand square in the mirror with your centerline facing you in Passive Defensive Stance. Keep your hands down at your sides and throw a spear hand from this position. Do you feel comfortable and balanced? Avoid tension prior to striking, yet remain ready to strike.

Experiment with the five stances presented in this book and see which one you feel most comfortable and balanced in. Which one allows you to be the most relaxed, balanced, and deceptive before striking?

One-on-One

Now grab a partner and practice in front of each other. Practice using different stances and different hand positions and see if you can make very light contact with each other. Use an open and relaxed palm and not a closed fist. Practice this with respect and safety toward each other, and think of it as a light game of tag. Remember, it is important to have people to practice with, and if you don't respect your partners, people will not want to practice with you.

Make sure you are moving. You do not want to stay still and static. Experiment with more natural arm positions. Keep in mind that an open hand looks less threatening than a closed fist. (Figure 2–2a) Perhaps lay your hand on your chest or open your arms while you are talking and gesture as if you are trying to make a point.

How to Use It

With the appropriate amount of practice, you will find yourself able to relax into a natural body

Figure 2-2a

position even though your intention is to deliver a devastating blow. You will be better at hiding your intention, which will give you the advantage of entering the attacker's personal safety zone without him or her even realizing it.

More important, by understanding body language, you can defuse a possible dispute without it ever developing into a physical confrontation.

Often someone will threaten, expecting to see a physical response from you. If you respond in a relaxed, friendly, or nondescript manner, it can surprise the opponent enough that he or she abandons the attack. It also gives you the advantage of gaining control of the situation and the ability to respond to it as *you* see fit.

The more you practice this and the more you practice this with different partners, the better your "poker face" will become.

In Summary

You have become aware of the need to read and disguise telegraphs in order to use practical Kung Fu street defense. This skill takes effort and practice, but it is worth every ounce of energy you put into it. This skill will allow you to avoid becoming someone else's punching bag. It will give you the ability to strike when you see fit and deliver the most effective strike possible if you choose to do so.

Chapter 3

Stun, Crippling, and Knockout Shots

"Stun," "crippling," and "knockout" are strong words and bring up strong images in a person's mind. The type of force you respond with during an attack depends on your strategy or the end result you want to accomplish.

Every situation is different, and practical Kung Fu street defense emphasizes meeting the attack with the appropriate amount of force. Do not make the mistake of thinking that an assault with the intent to kill can be countered with a one-fingered technique to just the right point on the body. Again, this is nothing more than movie magic and has nothing to do with reality-based personal defense.

Real street defense can get dirty and ugly, but remember, you aren't the one who wants to bang someone over the head because you need another fix. You aren't the one trying to take someone's life without provocation.

Learning how to apply either a stun, crippling, or knockout shot gives you the means to stop an attacker who has both your lives in your hands. We're talking about both of you living to see another day and your attacker having an experience that might help change his or her ways.

Your Arsenal

Your arsenal is the tools you have on hand to counter with. This means the techniques you can use should you choose to attack. For most people, this would be their hands and feet. There are a number of ways to hold your hands, use your arms, and utilize your legs and feet that are effective when striking without causing you an undue amount of damage on impact.

We are going to cover what they are briefly, so you understand what they are and how they come out. We will then teach you how to use your body to deliver the most effective and forceful blow.

Pay attention to how you hold your hands and feet. It does make a difference. If you decide to strike and you break a knuckle or ankle on impact, you've just eliminated one of your weapons in your arsenal, giving your attacker a distinct advantage.

Keep in mind that these are just a few select basic punches, kicks, and strikes that are somewhat universal among most fighting arts. Ultimately, how you apply them will reflect on how you train.

Hand Techniques

We make a fist by rolling the fingers tightly and making sure the thumb is tucked but on the outside of the rolled fingers. (Figures 3–1a–c)

Forefist Strike

The forefist strike is nothing more than a straight punch. As the punch extends from the body and the fist is released from the guard position, the fist rotates and turns over so the thumb is facing down. (Figures 3–1d–f) The fist rotation in this strike is most prevalent in the jab (Figures 3–1g–i) or reverse punch. (Figures 3–1j–l)

Vertical Punch

The vertical punch is similar to the forefist strike, but with no rotation of the fist. It is a straight punch that lands with the thumb turned upward toward the ceiling. (Figures 3–1m–o)

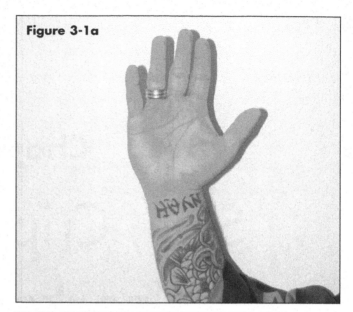

Figure 3-1a

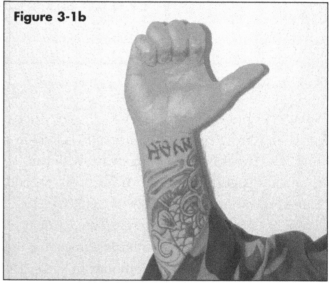

Figure 3-1b

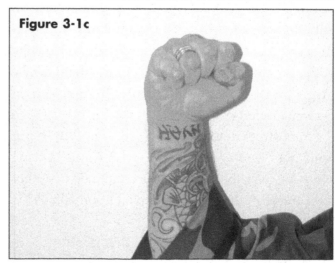

Figure 3-1c

Figure 3-1d

Figure 3-1g

Figure 3-1e

Figure 3-1h

Figure 3-1f

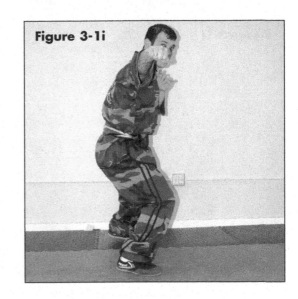

Figure 3-1i

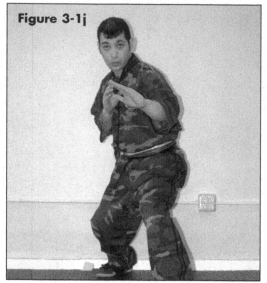

Figure 3-1j

Figure 3-1m

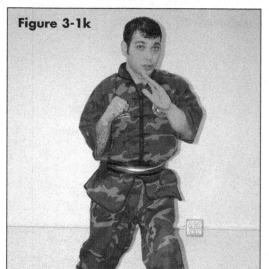

Figure 3-1k

Figure 3-1n

Figure 3-1l

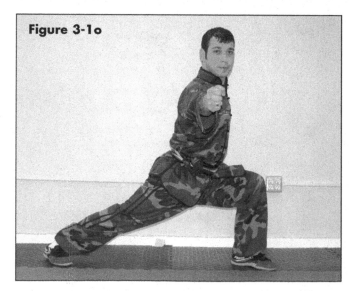

Figure 3-1o

Back Fist

The back fist is a punch that swings out like a door in an arching motion from the guard position. This back fist is known as the speed back fist or the "Chinese jab." Like a good Western boxing jab, speed is everything; the speed creates power on this strike. Also like the Western jab it can be used to bridge an attacker, countering or forcefully snapping an attacker's head back. This technique hinges from the elbow and the knuckles land to deliver the blow. (Figure 3–1p–r)

Hammer Fist

There are several hammer fist strikes. Here, for simplicity's sake, we only cover the basic hammer fist hand position, which is applied with the same basic mechanics of the speed back fist. This technique uses the side of the fist that runs below the little finger when landing. Make a tight fist and strike with the bottom of it like a hammer. It also is executed with an arching motion from the guard position. (Figures 3–1s–v)

Knife Hand

In the knife hand, the fingers are uncurled and next to each other with the thumb tucked in, locking the fingers straight. You strike with the side of the fist below the little finger. The palm can be either up or down. This technique also hinges outward from the elbow. This technique works very well when applied to the jugular vein. (Figures 3–1w–z)

Figure 3-1p

Figure 3-1r

Figure 3-1q

Figure 3-1s

Figure 3-1t

Figure 3-1u

Figure 3-1v

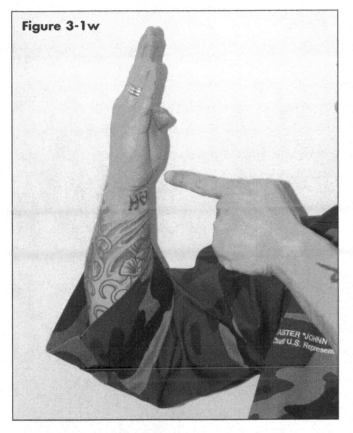

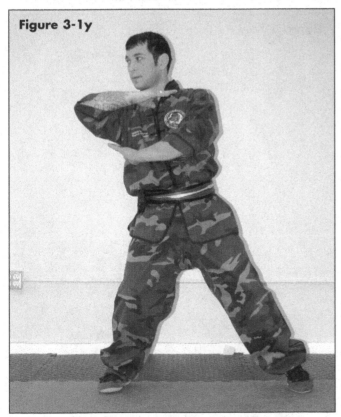

Figure 3-1w

Figure 3-1x

Figure 3-1y

Figure 3-1z

Spear Hand

In the spear hand, the hand position is the same as the knife hand, except the hand rotates as it strikes. This is a straight-line attack similar to the forefist strike. On impact the palm is facing down and the tips of the fingers are used to make contact. Again locking the fingers straight. To avoid finger jamming, this strike should only be used on eyes gauges and throat shots. The spear hand is also as speed strike, mainly used for stunning your opponent. Danger: this can blind or kill someone and should only be used under extreme circumstances. (Figures 3–1aa–ff.)

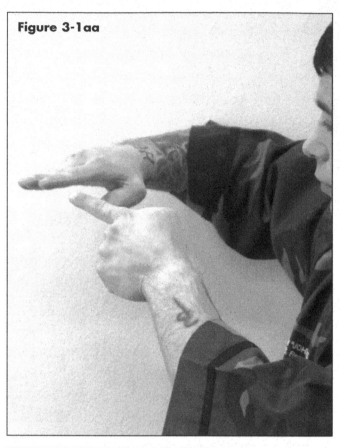

Figure 3-1aa

Figure 3-1bb

Figure 3-1cc

Figure 3-1dd

Figure 3-1ee

Figure 3-1ff

Tiger's Mouth

In the tiger's mouth, once again the fingers are together, but this time the thumb is out. (Figure 3-1gg) This is also a straight-line attack with the palm facing down. The striking surface is the ridge along the index finger and thumb. Your target will be the Adam's apple or throat—driving your hand straight underneath and behind the throat, grabbing, squeezing, and ripping back in a pulling motion. Danger: this can kill someone and should only be used under extreme circumstances. (Figures 3–1gg–ll)

Elbow Strike

In the elbow strike, the arm is bent and the bony surface of the elbow is used to strike. Shown here is the cutting elbow, which is a circular strike with a snap elbow strike that is a straight attack. Both strikes can be used from the second, third, and fourth range. (Figures 3–1mm–pp)

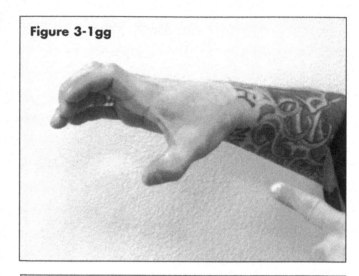

Figure 3-1gg

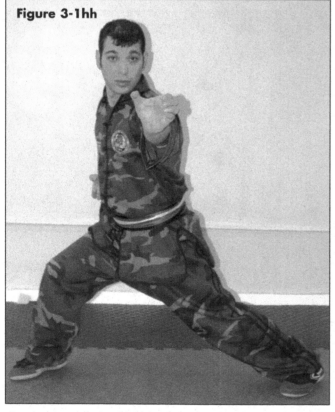

Figure 3-1hh

Figure 3-1ii

28

Figure 3-1jj

Figure 3-1kk

Figure 3-1ll

Figure 3-1mm

Figure 3-1nn

Figure 3-1oo

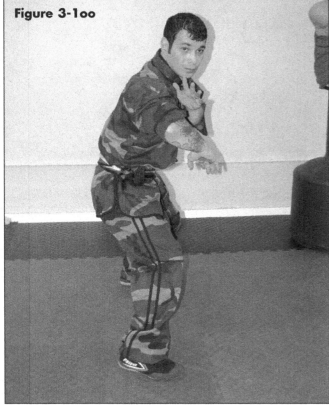

Figure 3-1pp

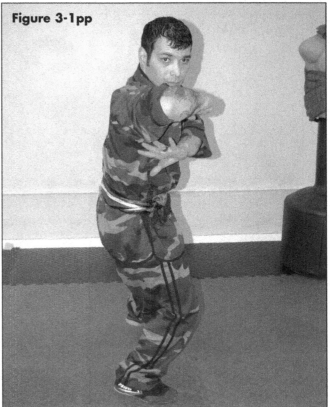

Leg Techniques

If you elect to use the legs and feet to attack, do not use your toes to strike. Only the dense bony surfaces of the foot should be used: instep, knife edge (side of the foot), or bottom of the heel. Proper form generates power and also makes it hard for an opponent to grab your foot or leg. Although they build balance and flexibility, high kicks are not important in street defense. Kicks to the ribs, bladder, groin, and legs work best in real combat. Remember, a kick is an extension of the knee. So if you are too close to kick, knee away. Also, if you are going to kick someone in the face, double them over first. It works better.

Front Snap Kick

Aim at the groin with this kick. In the front snap kick, the knee lifts and the lower leg extends forward from the knee. The striking surface is the instep. (Figures 3–2a–e)

Front Stomp Kick

In the front stomp kick, the knee lifts and the leg thrusts straight down. The bottom of the foot or the bottom of the heel makes contact with the opponent. Aim at the front or side of the knee and shin with this kick. It can be used to finish a downed attacker. (Figures 3–2f–j)

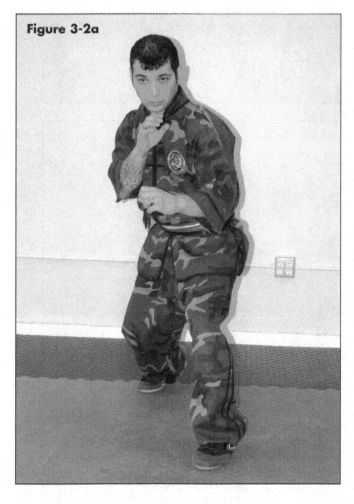

Figure 3-2a

Figure 3-2b

Figure 3-2c

Figure 3-2d

Figure 3-2e

Figure 3-2f

Figure 3-2g

Figure 3-2h

Figure 3-2i

Figure 3-2j

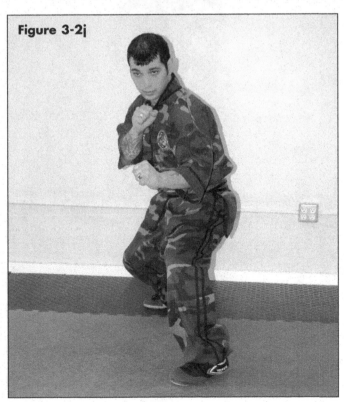

Side Snap Kick

In the side snap kick, the knee lifts and rotates. The leg thrusts to the side, making contact with the bottom of the foot or the side edge of the foot. (Figures 3–2k–o.)

Side Stomp Kick

In the side stomp kick, the knee lifts and the leg thrusts straight down and to the side. The bottom of the foot or the bottom of the heel makes contact with the opponent. (Figures 3–2p–t)

Knee Strike

In the knee strike, the leg is bent, the knee lifts, and the bony surface of the knee is used to strike with. (Figures 3-2u–w.)

These are simple techniques used to counter an opponent. In practical Kung Fu street defense, where you strike is of the utmost importance. The emphasis is on economy of movement, or the least amount of effort with the greatest amount of impact. Different types of impact can be made. Moving forward, we will discuss the type of force you choose to respond with and the repercussions of each type.

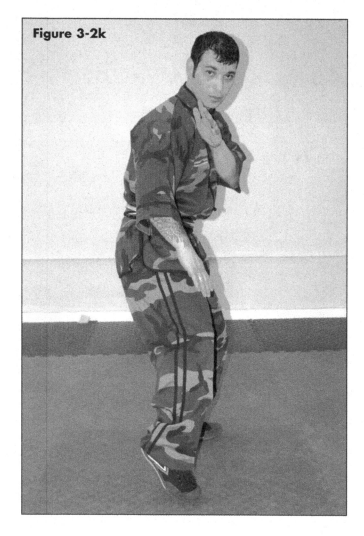

Figure 3-2k

Figure 3-2l

Figure 3-2m

Figure 3-2n

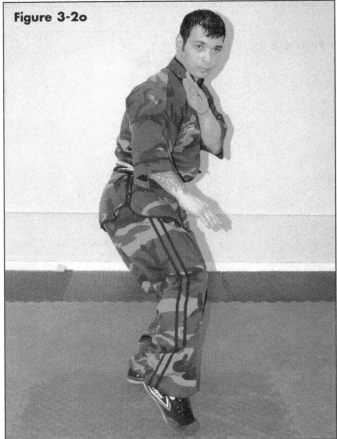

Figure 3-2o

Figure 3-2p

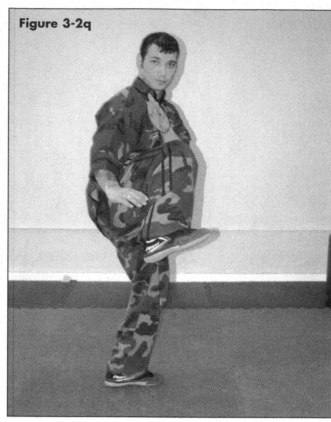

Figure 3-2q

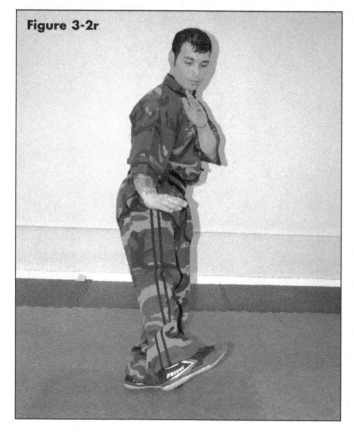

Figure 3-2r

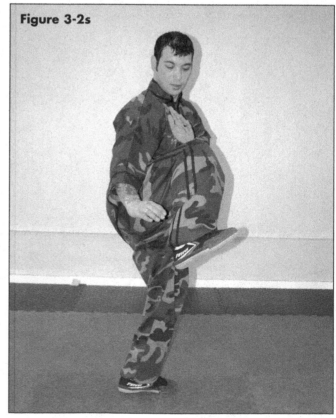

Figure 3-2s

Figure 3-2t

Figure 3-2u

Figure 3-2v

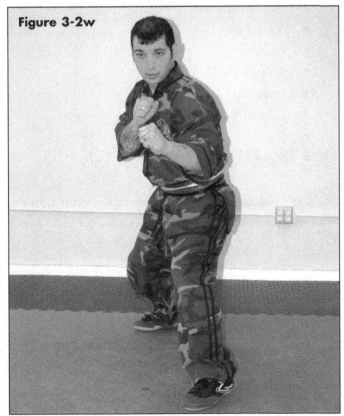

Figure 3-2w

Target Areas

Target areas are vulnerable spots on the body. They tend to be soft and fairly unprotected by bone and large tissue. This vulnerability makes any kind of impact in these areas painful and debilitating.

These susceptible areas tend to be cavities, areas on the body where internal organs are close to the surface, places where bones hinge together, places where tendons attach to bone, or spaces where nerve endings are clustered.

Following is a list of target areas:

- eyes
- nose
- temple
- hinge of the jaw
- throat
- solar plexus (abdominal nerves)
- bladder
- groin
- base of the skull
- collarbone
- kidneys
- coccyx (tailbone)
- kneecap
- side of the knee
- shin
- instep

Consult any basic anatomy diagram if you are unsure where some of these areas are.

How to Stun

To "stun" means to stop someone in their tracks, to have them take notice and change intent, to surprise them with an unexpected consequence. In other words, you are trying to make a point and nothing more.

How to Cripple

To "cripple" in this context doesn't mean to maim, it means to strike with the type of force that makes the adversary completely incapable of delivering another blow or another potent strike. Your counter makes them unwilling to pursue the attack any further because of the pain or incapacity they are experiencing.

How to Knock Out

To "knock out" means just that—to make the opponent unconscious for complete cessation of the attack.

Note: There are plenty of manuals filled with killer military-type techniques out there. This book is not meant to be one of them. This is merely a practical self-defense guide, with the goal of sharing enough useful information that can you survive a street attack.

Chapter 4

Evade, Parry, and Block

This book provides you with an arsenal of techniques to effectively handle a threatening situation, but the best way to preserve your life is to not let a situation escalate to that level, if possible.

With that said, we will discuss three aspects of defensive fighting that will either get you out of the way or help you effectively deflect potentially lethal strikes. They are evade, parry, and block.

Evade

Let's get back to a very simple basic concept—move! Evade means nothing more than to get out of the way. There is never any reason to stand in the line of an attack. It is important not to let the first strike land. If it does, you are at a distinct disadvantage. Evading also gives you an opportunity to decide how you want to respond and the amount of force you want to use.

We talked about the concept of getting out of the way in chapter 1 when you were first learning about stance work. Evading is taking it up to the next level. You apply the same concepts in a more dynamic way with more confidence and commitment.

What It Develops

As you become more adept at evading, you will be lighter and quicker on your feet. You will step more efficiently, and you will learn how to bob and weave.

How to Use It

Here is another drill you could work immediately at real speed and as fast as possible. It is nothing more than a refined game of tag, but will help you learn how to evade, step to the angles, and get out of the way. You will also get a realistic feel for the different combat ranges.

Stand in front of a friend in either a Fighting Cat Stance or Passive Defensive Stance. (Figure 4–1a) Decide who is "it" and have that person continually try to step in and touch the other person at the center of his or her chest. This should be done quickly and with intention. Confine the area you are working in to a 12-square-foot area so no one is tempted to start running around.

The person who is evading should stay light on the feet while turning the centerline out of the way of each attack. Work the angles.

Figure 4-1a

Parry

Even the fastest person can get caught in a fight. A parry is the next level of defense and is your first insurance policy against an offensive strike making full contact. A parry is a slight deflection of the incoming strike. It can be used on its own or can be used to set up a retaliatory combination.

A parry is used with an open palm and the fingers together and thumb tucked in. To parry, bring your hand down on the strike or bat the punch to the side. It is used as you evade the attack and in combination with the fact that you are repositioning yourself. You can reposition yourself to completely get out of the way or reposition yourself to counterattack.

What It Develops

The parry helps you develop the ability to move and roll with an attack so you don't accept its full force. It allows you to stay in combat range #2 where you can effectively control your opponent,

counter efficiently, and counter with the appropriate force.

How to Use It

Go back to the drill of Kung Fu tag. This time, as your partner steps in to touch your centerline, work on parrying the attack either down or to the side. Parry close to the wrist or forearm.

Start this exercise a bit slower and work up to full speed as you become more proficient and comfortable with it. It is important to work at full speed to truly understand how to parry effectively.

Block

Sometimes a parry just isn't enough. A block is the next level of defense and is your last insurance policy against an offensive strike making full contact. A block is a complete deflection of the incoming strike. It can be used on its own, or it can be used to set up a retaliatory combination.

There is a saying that goes, "A block is a strike and a strike is a block." Get into the mind-set that a block should be used with as much force as a punch or kick. Don't fall into the mind-set that if you just hit hard enough you can fend off anything.

Once again, we cannot stress enough that if the first blow of attack lands, you are at a distinct disadvantage. You must learn to block with as much force and intention as a good counterattack.

Blocking Techniques

Most blocks are executed by using the outer or inner surface of the bony and fleshy parts of the forearm. Regardless, it is still important that you keep your hand in a tight fist to protect your fingers and to help keep the forearm muscles engaged.

Effective blocking relies on a last-minute torque or twisting of the forearm to take striking advantage of the momentum of the incoming attack. It also is important to understand where to stop the block. Blocking too wide and too far from the body will give your opponent openings to attack.

High Block

The high block is used against anything attacking the area above the shoulders. The forearm crosses the centerline of the chest and then lifts and rotates up until it is off the crown of the head at a slight angle from the forehead. The blocking surface is the outer edge or your forearm; you should finish pinky side. (Figures 4–3a–c)

Figure 4-3a

Figure 4-3b

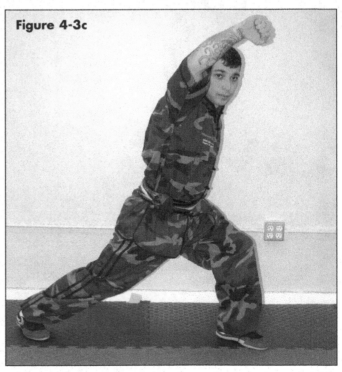

Figure 4-3c

Middle Block

The middle block is used against anything coming in to the middle of the body. The forearm crosses the centerline of the chest and then moves to the side. A right middle block would move to the right. A left middle block would move to the left. It is important the block stops slightly past the rib cage with the elbow a couple of inches away from the body. The blocking surface is the inside of your forearm, so you finish thumbside out. (Figure 4–3d–f)

Figure 4-3d

Figure 4-3e

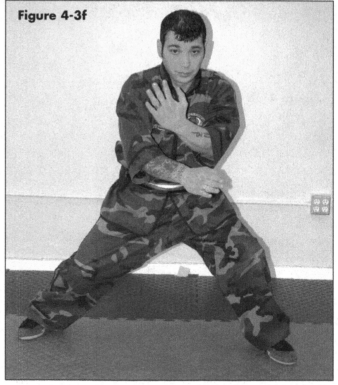

Figure 4-3f

Outside Middle Block

The outside middle block is used against anything coming in to the middle of the body. The forearm crosses the centerline of the chest and then torques as it moves to the side. A right outside middle block would move to the right. A left outside middle block would move to the left. It is important that the block stops slightly past the rib cage with the elbow a couple of inches away from the body. The forearm torques outward and the palm should stop facing away from you. (Figures 4–3g–i)

Figure 4-3g

Figure 4-3h

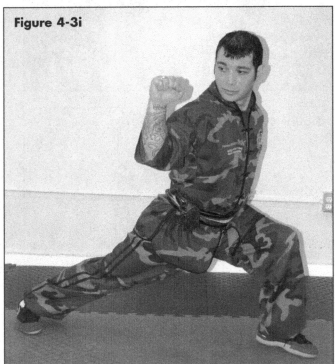

Figure 4-3i

Cross Middle Block

The cross middle block is used against anything coming in to the middle of the body. The forearm lifts to the side of the body, torques, and crosses the centerline of the chest. A right cross middle block would start at the right and move to the left.

A left cross middle block would start at the left and move to the right. It is important the block stops slightly past the rib cage with the elbow a couple of inches away from the body. The forearm torques inward. When the block is completed the palm should be facing you. (Figures 4–3j–m)

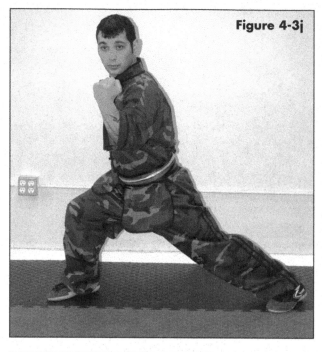

Figure 4-3j

Figure 4-3k

Figure 4-3l

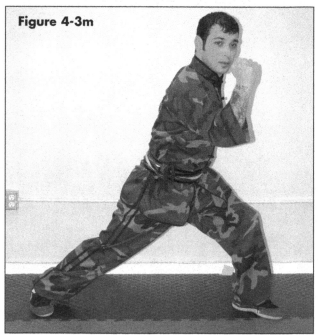

Figure 4-3m

Downward Block

The downward block is used against anything attacking below the waist and above the mid-thigh. This block is the only one where the fist or palm drops straight down to execute the block. (Figures 4–3n–q.)

Figure 4-3o

Figure 4-3n

Figure 4-3p

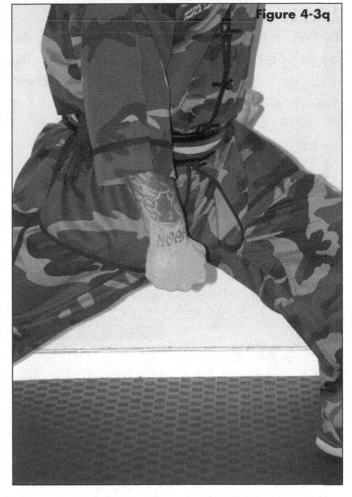

Figure 4-3q

How to Use It

Stand in front of a friend in either a Fighting Cat Stance or Passive Defensive Stance. One person is the attacker, the other is working the blocks. The person who is the attacker should step out into the Bow and Arrow Stance throwing a forefist strike to the centerline. The person working the blocks practices executing the various blocks as your partner punches.

Start slow and work yourself up to a realistic speed. Always keep in mind that as you become faster, the potential for serious harm increases. While practicing, the attacker's punch should stop an inch or two from your partner without making any contact.

High Block

In the high block, the attacker punches to the center of the face or swings overhead. Step to the angle as the block crosses the center of the chest, torques, and rises to move the attacking arm out of the way. The block must come into contact underneath the opponent's arm.

Middle Block

In the middle block, the attacker punches to the center of the body. Step to the angle as the block crosses the center of the chest and moves the attacking arm out of the way. The block must come into contact with the side of the opponent's arm.

Outside Middle Block

In the outside middle block, the attacker punches to the center of the body. Step to the angle as the block crosses the center of the chest, torques, and moves the attacking arm out of the way. The block must come into contact with the side of the opponent's arm.

Cross Middle Block

In the cross middle block, the attacker punches to the center of the body. Step to an angle as the block crosses the center of the chest, torques, and moves the attacking arm out of the way. The block must come into contact with the side of the opponent's arm.

Downward Block

In the downward block, the attacker kicks to the center of the body below the waist. Shift to an angle as the block drops straight down. The block comes into contact with the top of the attacker's foot.

In Summary

Moving, deflecting, and blocking are the first components of a practical Kung Fu street defense counter. The ability to move out of the way of, deflect, or completely disarm an attacker's first line of fire will put you at a distinct advantage. It will give you a split second to decide exactly how you want to respond to an attack and how much force you want to use.

You have learned the importance of stances to build a strong foundation for practical Kung Fu street defense. You have an understanding of angles and combat ranges. You now have the ability to evade, parry, or block and an arsenal of effective hand and foot techniques to use on target areas that will allow you to stun, cripple, or knockout your attacker.

Practice is everything. If you are not currently active in the martial arts, I recommend that you find a credible school in your area and train. We put a lot of work into this book, but nothing can replace good live training with a capable instructor.

Let's put it all together and get to the real heart and soul of practical Kung Fu street defense.

Chapter 5

The Warrior Mentality

Physically, a person can learn just about anything. Everyone can learn how to punch. Some people will punch more accurately right away. Others will need more practice to hit a target effectively. The difference between two people's ability is the amount of time they need to repeat something to become proficient in what they are trying to do.

The same applies to blocks, grabs, kicks, etc. Continual improvement can be accomplished through repetition.

No matter how capable a person becomes in physical application, one component must be present to respond appropriately to an attack. We call it the warrior mentality.

Accessing the Survival Instinct

You must not be afraid to attack the attack. A full response is necessary to disable someone intent on causing you harm.

All martial art application is 50 percent physical and 50 percent psychological. No matter how effective your form or style, if you are incapable of pulling the mental trigger behind your techniques, they will ultimately be useless.

This means you must have the confidence and conviction to avoid or shut down an attack before it is right on top of you. You must believe in your ability to move in at angles, parry, block, jam, and hit.

The confidence and conviction to react in this way is part of our survival instinct. Unfortunately, as we mature, many of us have learned to question or shut off many of our more primal or "gut" instincts.

It is imperative that your mind is in tune with your body and that they act as one. A moment's hesitation from either can cost you everything.

How to Access the Warrior Mentality

This is a thought experiment you can do to feel the different mind-sets a person might experience during an attack. Read through this and then play with the idea. It is important that you truly try to put yourself in these scenarios to understand the emotional context we are discussing.

Close your eyes and imagine you are walking down a dimly lit street at night. You are slightly lost and you turn left and find yourself at a dead end. You turn to retrace your steps and see two dark images appear. They are walking in your direction. One is holding what looks like a bat.

Put yourself in this situation and sit with the emotions you are feeling. Think about how your gut feels. Are your muscles tensing? Do you feel confused as to what you should do?

Open your eyes again and clear your mind.

Now once again imagine you are walking down a dimly lit street at night. If you are a parent, imagine you are with your child. Or your wife or husband. Or anyone for whom you have a deep affection. As you turn the corner, two men jump out from a darkened storefront to block your path. It looks like one is holding a knife and is approaching your loved one.

Sit with the emotions this situation conjures up. How does it compare to when you imagined you were alone?

Often we will respond with more ferocity when a loved one is threatened as compared to ourselves. That kind of ferocity must be present under all threatening situations, ready to be accessed when you decide to pull the trigger on your defense.

If You Snooze, You Lose

Do not wait for an attack. As soon as a threat becomes real…*act!* Trust your gut. It *will* tell you when a threat is present. Self-defense is not about trading blows back and forth. Trading blows back and forth is called fighting. Fighting is not what you are learning to do with this book.

Self-defense is about protecting oneself by any means necessary. If you truly feel threatened, strike first, hard, and accurately with one goal in mind: to keep yourself protected from the aggressive source of violence that found its way to you.

This is so important for successful self-defense that we are going to say it again. It is imperative that your mind is in tune with your body and that they act as one. A moment's hesitation from either one can cost you everything.

Self-Defense

Violence should always be a last resort. Seek peaceful ways to resolve conflict, but remember, if your soul is threatened, let your soul become a warrior.

There are times when violence becomes unavoidable. To be prepared both mentally and physically when this happens, train the way you would want your techniques to come out on the street. Envision yourself in combat with every punch and kick you throw. If you practice in this manner, bringing your mind and full intention into every move, every application, it *will* come out—it *will* be there, if you should ever need it.

Kung Fu is beautiful. Fighting is ugly. Combat is never pretty, no matter what you hear or what you see in the movies. Always remember that, prepare, and train hard.

Chapter 6

Defense against a Punch

This chapter will outline different ways to defend against a punch. A punch is the most common form of attack and is the type of offensive technique most people are naturally inclined to throw. It is the easiest attack for most people to execute, so a punch is used in all types of situations, from the random street attack, to altercations at social events, to domestic violence.

Regardless of the circumstance, this chapter will show you how to effectively avoid, parry, or block this common form of attack and then follow through with the appropriate response.

Technique A

Tsai engages the opponent.

The opponent throws a reverse
punch and Tsai counters.

Tsai delivers a palm heel strike to the face.

Technique A continued

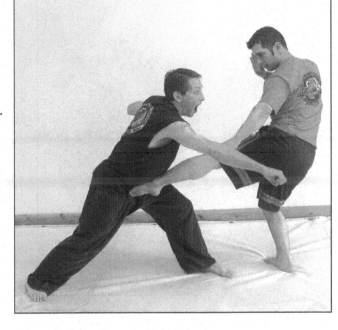

Tsai executes a roundhouse kick to the groin.

Tsai finishes the opponent with a cutting punch to the jaw.

Technique B

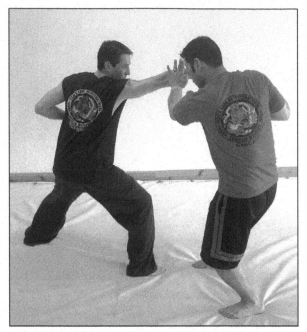

The opponent throws a lunge punch and Tsai deflects the attack.

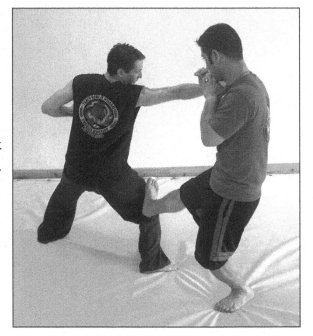

Tsai executes a front kick to the opponent's knee.

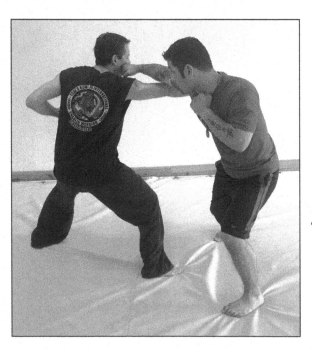

Tsai throws a cutting punch to the jaw.

Technique B continued

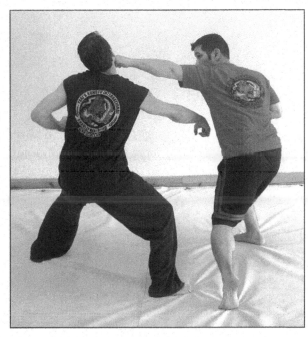

Tsai throws a second punch
with the opposite arm.

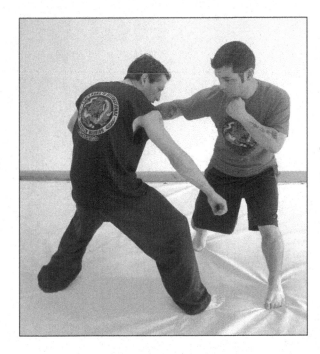

Tsai finishes with a punch
to the solar plexus.

Technique C

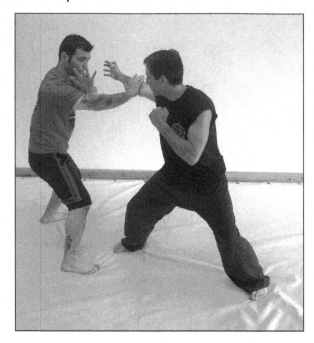

The opponent throws a lunging grab and Tsai deflects the attack.

Tsai throws a back fist to the temple.

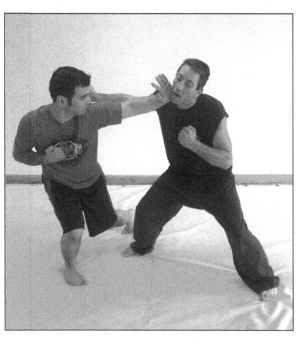

Tsai throws a palm heel strike to the jaw.

Technique C continued

Tsai throws a hook punch to the solar plexus.

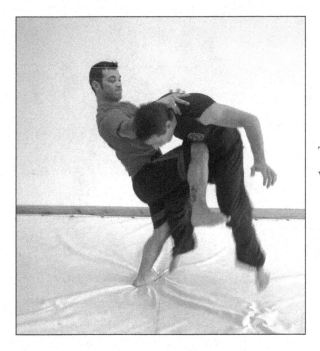

Tsai finishes off the opponent
with a knee to the body.

Technique D

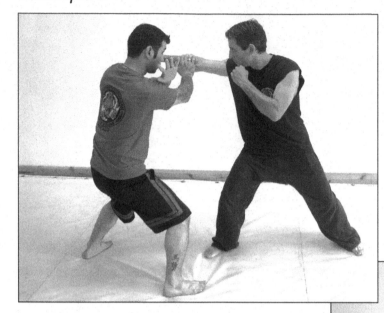

The opponent throws a jab and Tsai deflects the attack.

Tsai strikes the opponent with a forearm strike.

Tsai delivers a knife hand to the jaw.

Technique D continued

Tsai delivers a hook punch to the opposite side of the jaw.

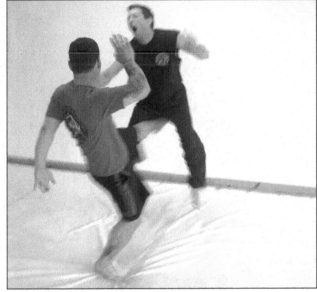

Tsai finishes with a front snap kick to the groin.

Technique E

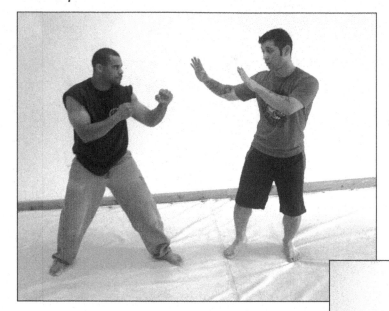

Tsai engages the opponent.

The opponent throws a reverse punch which Tsai counters with a side kick.

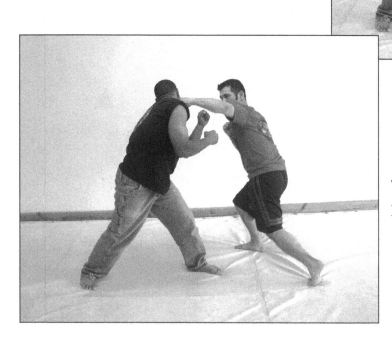

Tsai steps forward and delivers a cutting punch.

Technique E continued

Tsai executes a roundhouse kick.

Tsai finishes the opponent with a cutting punch to the jaw.

Technique F

Tsai is confronted by the attacker.

The attacker throws a hook punch which Tsai counters with an uppercut and block.

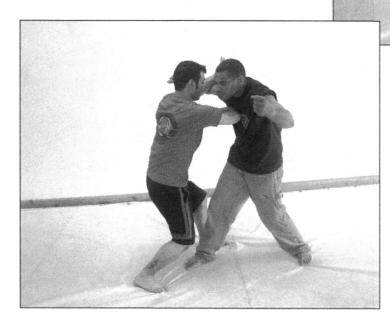

Tsai elbows the opponent in the solar plexus.

Technique F continued

Tsai strikes to the groin.

Tsai reaches around the attacker's head and delivers a knee strike.

Technique G

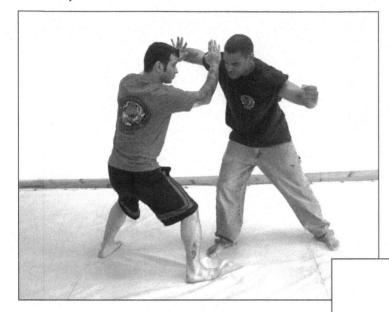

The attacker throws a hook punch and Tsai blocks the strike using both hands.

Tsai delivers a knife hand to the neck.

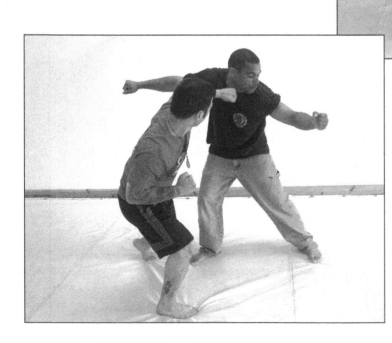

Tsai hook punches the attacker.

Technique G continued

Tsai throws an uppercut to
the jaw of the attacker.

Tsai finishes the attacker with a
front snap kick to the groin.

Technique H

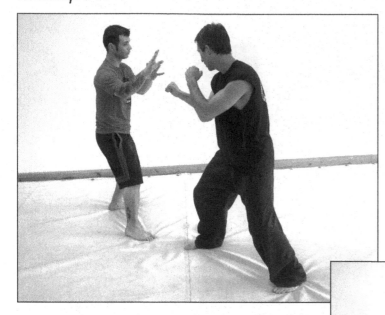

Tsai is confronted by the attacker.

The attacker throws a jab while Tsai counters with an elbow strike to the ribs.

Tsai counters with a hook punch to the same ribs.

Technique H continued

Tsai steps behind and strikes the attacker in the jaw.

Tsai takes the attacker to the ground.

Technique I

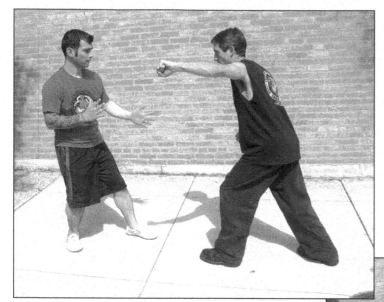

The attacker throws a lunge punch at Tsai.

Tsai blocks the strike.

Tsai counters with a front stomp kick to the knee.

Technique I continued

Tsai steps to the outside while delivering a strike to the temple.

Tsai finishes the attacker with a right-hand cutting punch.

Reverse angle of strike.

Technique J

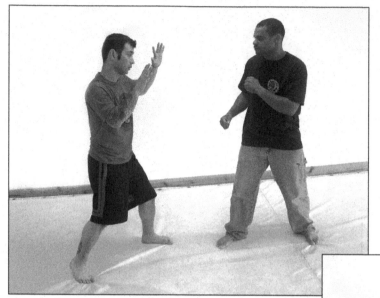

Tsai is confronted by the attacker.

The attacker throws a hook punch and Tsai blocks the strike.

Tsai counters with a front thrust kick.

Technique J continued

Tsai delivers a vertical punch to the jaw.

Tsai finishes the attacker
with a reverse punch.

Technique K

The attacker throws a hook punch at Tsai while he counters with a lunge punch.

The attacker throws a jab and Tsai deflects the counter.

The attacker throws a left hook punch.

Technique K continued

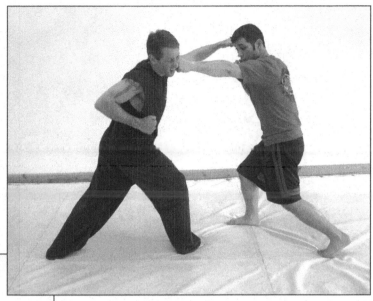

Tsai counters with a straight punch to the attacker's nose.

Tsai finishes the attacker with a round-house to the body.

Technique L

The attacker throws a left jab at Tsai's head. Tsai deflects the punch to the inside.

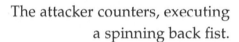

The attacker counters, executing a spinning back fist.

Tsai blocks the spinning back fist at the wrist and just behind the elbow.

Technique L continued

Tsai creates an armbar.

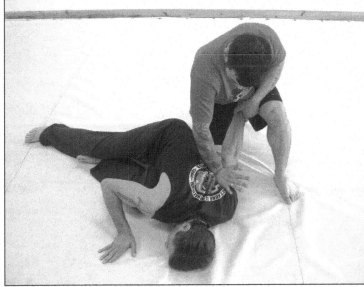

Tsai takes the attacker to the ground.

Chapter 7

Defense against a Kick

In this chapter, we show defensive techniques designed to stop leg attacks. An assault rarely starts with a kick, but kicking techniques pack more power and, when executed properly, can be devastating to the recipient. Most of the time, leg techniques are used as a follow-through for the first strike.

You will learn how to neutralize a leg before it can do harm. Building the confidence that you can stop a kick goes a long way to defending against this type of attack. Follow the techniques laid out in this chapter to build competence against this kind of variable.

Technique A

Tsai and the attacker square off.

The attacker executes a high roundhouse kick while Tsai counters by adding a front snap to the groin.

Technique B

Tsai and opponent square off.

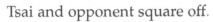

The attacker attempts to execute a front snap kick and Tsai "checks" the kick.

Tsai steps forward and delivers a vertical punch to the attacker's jaw.

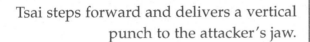

Technique B continued

Tsai throws a reverse punch to the opponent's body.

Tsai finishes with a roundhouse kick to the lower leg.

Technique C

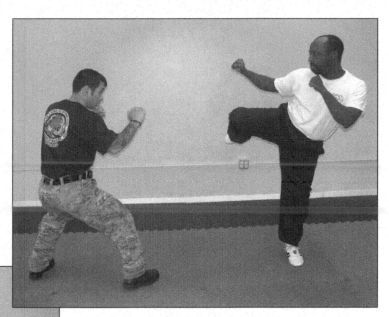

The attacker begins to execute a roundhouse kick.

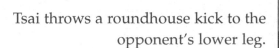

Tsai steps in and blocks the kick.

Tsai throws a roundhouse kick to the opponent's lower leg.

Technique C continued

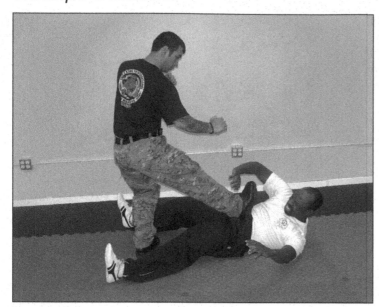

The attacker falls to the ground and Tsai delivers a stomp kick to the downed opponent.

Technique D

The attacker throws a roundhouse kick and Tsai blocks the kick.

Tsai counters with a front snap kick to the lower stomach.

Tsai steps down and delivers a jab.

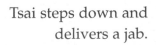

Technique D continued

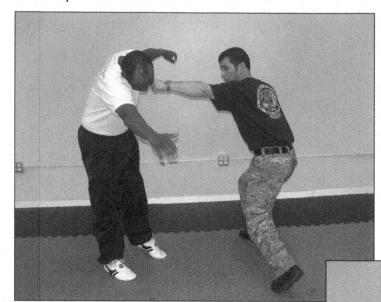

Tsai delivers a hook punch to the jaw.

The opponent is finished off with a roundhouse kick to the body.

Technique E

The opponent delivers a roundhouse kick while Tsai blocks the attacker.

Tsai counters with a groin kick.

Tsai steps forward to deliver a reverse punch to the opponent's jaw.

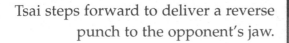

Technique E continued

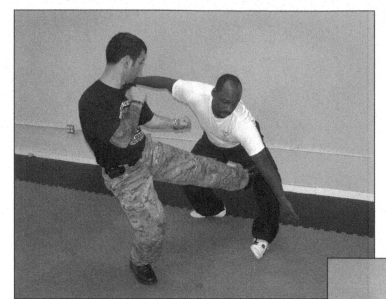

Tsai executes a roundhouse kick to the opponent's leg.

As the opponent falls to the ground, Tsai delivers a lunge punch to the neck.

Technique F

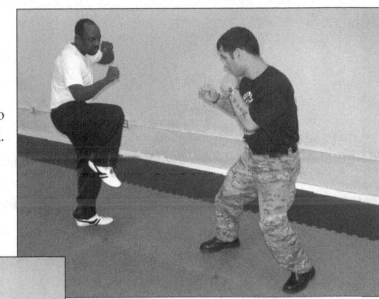

The opponent prepares to deliver a front snap kick.

Tsai counters with a punch to the foot.

Tsai slides forward and delivers a back fist.

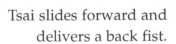

Technique F continued

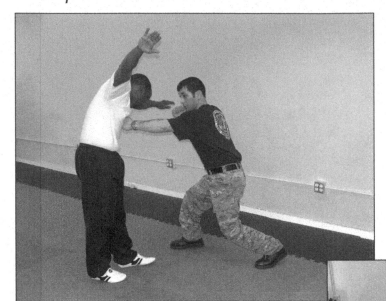

Tsai shifts his body weight to deliver a reverse punch.

Tsai delivers a knee to the opponent's solar plexus.

Technique G

The opponent delivers a side kick to Tsai.

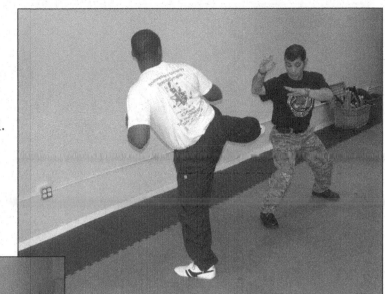

Tsai drops an elbow to the opponent's ankle.

Tsai slides forward.

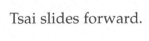

Technique G continued

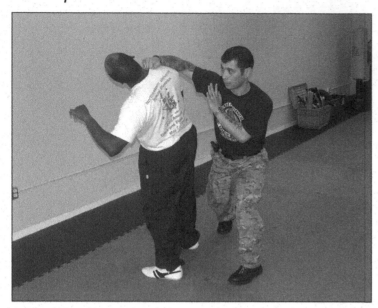

Tsai delivers a punch to the attacker's neck.

Technique H

The opponent delivers a side kick while Tsai steps to the outside of the kick.

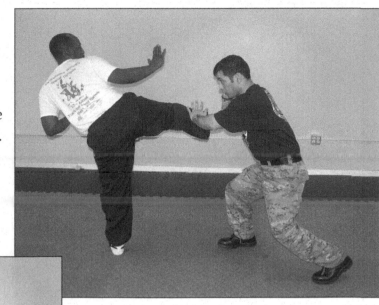

Tsai steps to the outside of the opponent while bringing his right hand around the opponent's neck.

Using his forearm to spin his attacker's chin, Tsai places the opponent in a sleeper hold.

Technique H continued

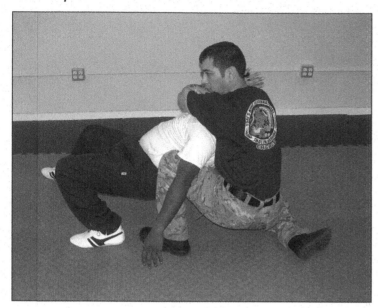

Dropping back, Tsai takes the opponent to the ground and chokes him out.

Technique 1

Tsai and opponent square off.

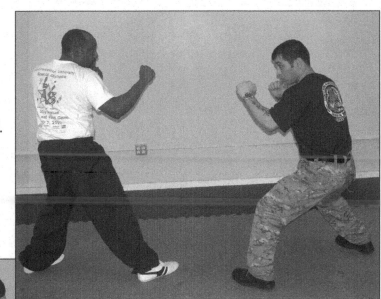

The attacker throws a reverse punch while Tsai deflects the attacker.

The attacker steps forward to deliver a lunge punch.

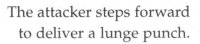

Technique I continued

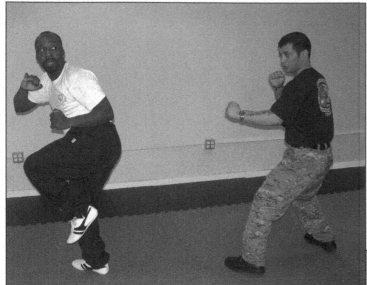

The attacker turns to execute a spinning back kick.

Tsai counters by delivering a front thrust kick to the spine before the attacker can execute his kick.

Technique J

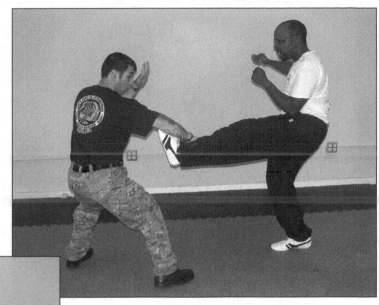

The attacker throws a front snap kick at Tsai.

The attacker steps down and executes a roundhouse kick. Tsai traps the leg under his left arm.

Tsai steps forward and prepares to sweep opponent's legs from under him.

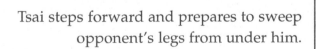

Technique J continued

Tsai kicks the opponent's base leg and strikes the chest.

The opponent is slammed to the ground.

Technique K

Tsai is trapped against a wall while the attacker executes a front thrust kick.

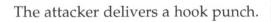

Tsai covers up to prepare for the impact of the kick.

The attacker delivers a hook punch.

Technique K continued

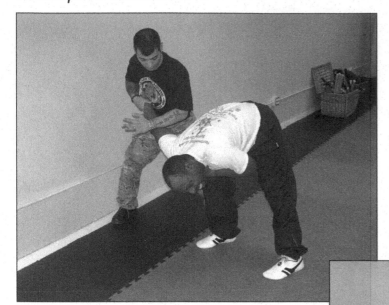

Tsai grabs the punch and turns the strike into an armbar.

Tsai finishes the counterattack with a front snap kick to the head.

Technique L

The attacker throws a roundhouse kick.

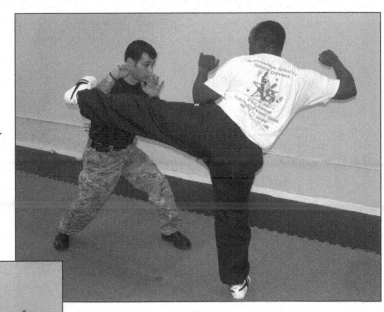

Tsai counters with a
low roundhouse of his own.

Tsai's kick causes the
opponent to fall to the ground.

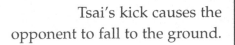

Technique L continued

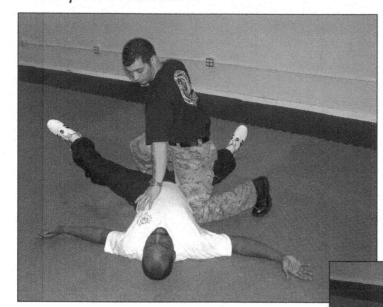

Tsai jumps on top of the opponent.

Tsai delivers a reverse
punch to the opponent's head.

Technique M

The opponent delivers a jab at Tsai.

The opponent rotates forward to deliver a reverse punch at Tsai.

The opponent delivers a roundhouse kick. Tsai counters with a front thrust kick.

Technique M continued

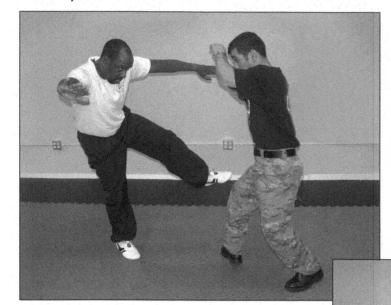

Tsai steps forward to prepare for an additional kick.

Tsai delivers a roundhouse kick to the opponent's floating ribs.

Technique N

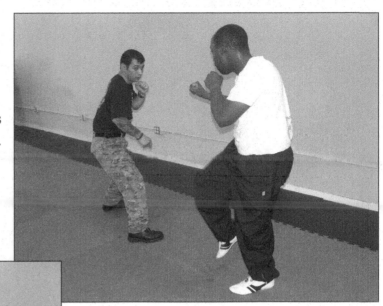

The opponent prepares
to deliver an axe kick.

Tsai deflects the opponent's kick.

Tsai slides forward and delivers a straight
punch to the solar plexus.

Technique N continued

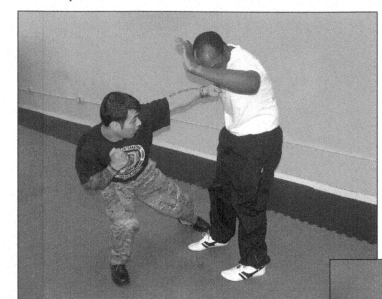

Tsai throws a fore fist punch to the sternum.

Tsai executes the finishing blow to the opponent's bladder.

Technique O

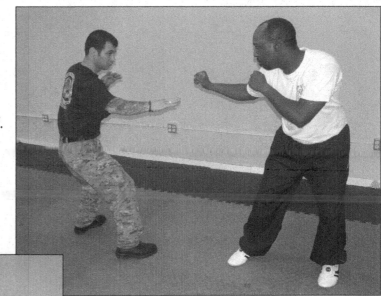

Tsai and attacker square off.

The attacker throws a side kick and Tsai attacks the striking leg with a forearm strike.

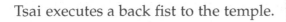

Tsai executes a back fist to the temple.

Technique O continued

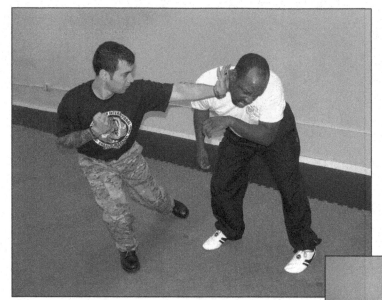

Tsai shifts his body weight and delivers a cutting palm-heel technique.

Tsai finishes the opponent with a front snap kick.

Chapter 8

Defense against a Grab

A grab is very common in street attacks. It can be used to initiate or to follow through. There are a number of things to do and not do when you find yourself on the end of a grab. With a better understanding of how the body moves and works, grabs can be effectively neutralized and countered.

Pay close attention to the angles presented in this chapter. Remember that striking with the proper intensity and accuracy is even more necessary to force your attacker to release you from a grab.

Technique A

An attacker grabs Tsai, and Tsai responds by grabbing the attacker's hand.

The attacker throws a hook punch at Tsai as he blocks with his left arm.

Tsai executes a palm strike with his right arm.

Technique A continued

Tsai delivers a knee strike to the attacker's midsection.

Tsai executes a right hook punch.

Technique B

The attacker walks down the street.

The attacker pins Tsai against the wall.

Tsai double slaps the attacker's ears, then places his arms around the attacker's neck.

Technique B continued

Tsai head butts the attacker.

Tsai rotates to his right and throws the attacker to the ground.

Technique C

The attacker engages Tsai.

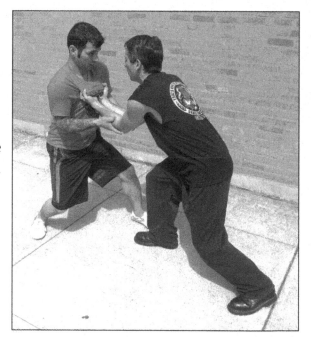

Tsai attacks two pressure points on the attacker's arms.

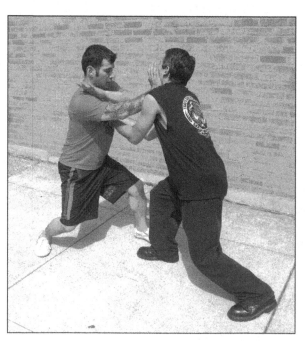

Tsai executes a palm heel strike to the attacker's jaw.

Technique C continued

Tsai executes a knife hand to the attacker's neck.

Technique D

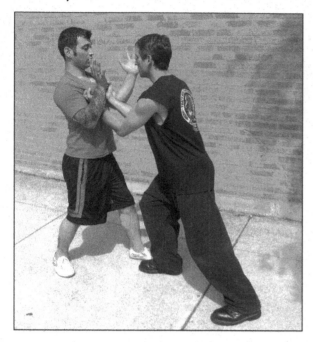

The attacker engages Tsai.

After trapping the attacker's hands,
Tsai attacks his attacker's eyes.

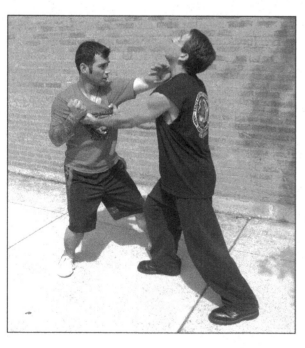

Tsai delivers a knife hand to the attacker's throat.

Technique D continued

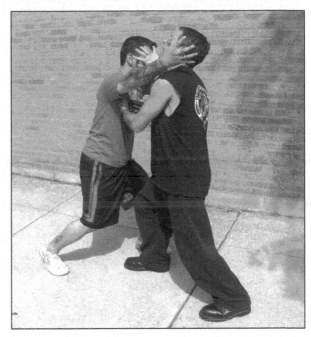

Tsai palm strikes the attacker's ear.

Tsai rotates the attacker's head.

Tsai takes his attacker to the ground.

Technique E

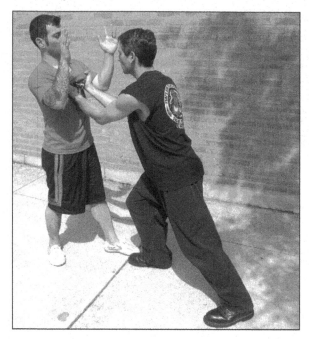

The attacker engages Tsai.

Tsai pushes the attacker's arms, pinning them together.

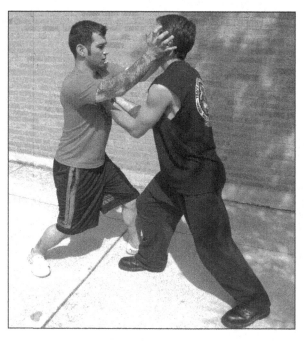

Tsai open palm slaps the attacker in both ears.

Technique E continued

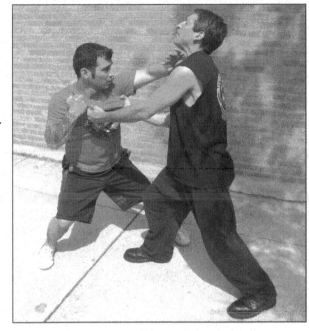

Tsai strikes the attacker in the throat.

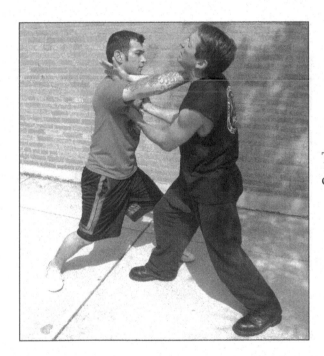

Tsai delivers an additional knife hand to the opposite side of his attacker's neck.

Tsai delivers a knife hand to the attacker's throat.

Technique F

Tsai and the attacker engage each other.

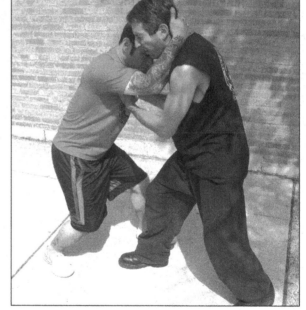

Tsai delivers a head butt to his attacker.

Tsai executes a knee to the attacker's ribs.

Technique F continued

Tsai throws the attacker to the ground.

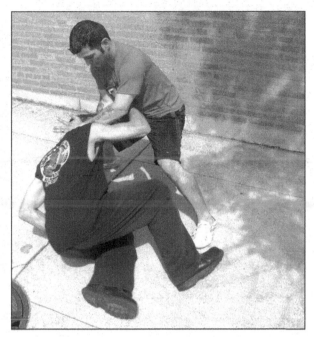

Tsai delivers a side kick to the attacker's face.

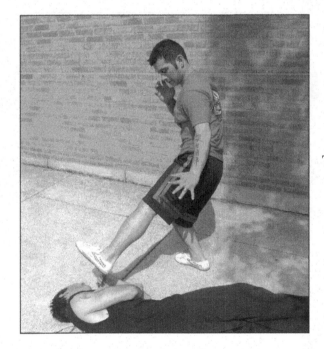

Technique G

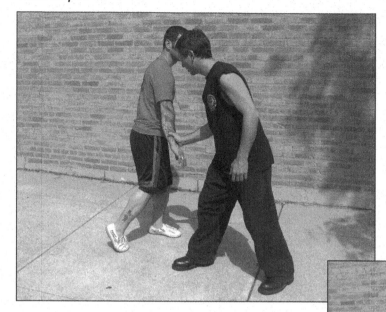

The attacker grabs Tsai's right arm.

Tsai rotates the attacker's arm clockwise.

Tsai places his left palm
on the attacker's elbow.

Technique G continued

Tsai delivers a roundhouse kick to
attacker's support leg.

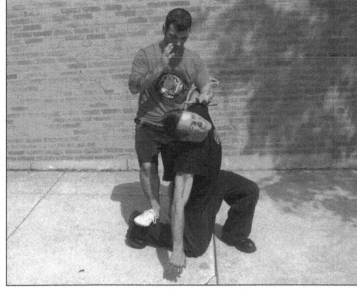

Tsai stomps on the attacker's ankle.

Technique H

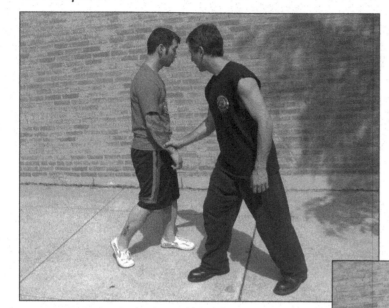

The attacker grabs Tsai's right arm.

Tsai rotates the attacker's arm counterclockwise, breaking free.

Tsai executes a ridge hand to the attacker's neck.

Technique H continued

Tsai executes a roundhouse kick to the attacker's leg.

Tsai stomps on the attacker's ankle.

Technique 1

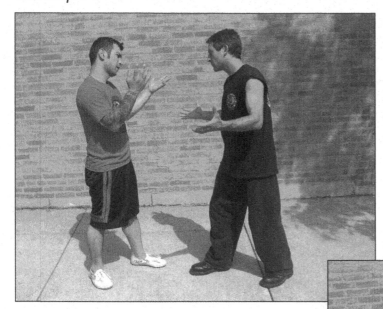

Tsai and the attacker engage each other in conversation.

The attacker grabs Tsai's right wrist. Tsai counters with a palm strike to the attacker's head.

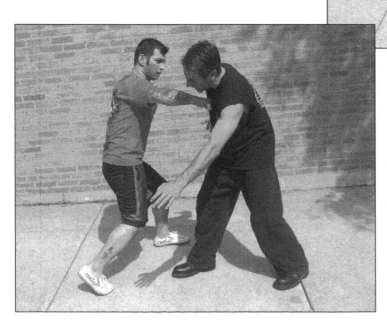

Tsai delivers a reverse punch to the attacker's chest.

Technique I continued

Tsai executes a back fist to the attacker's temple.

Tsai executes a vertical punch to the attacker's jaw.

Technique J

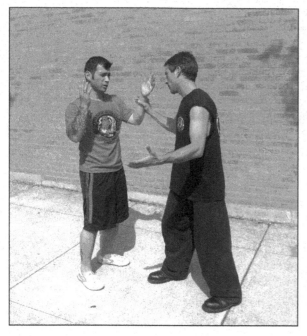

The attacker grabs Tsai's left wrist.

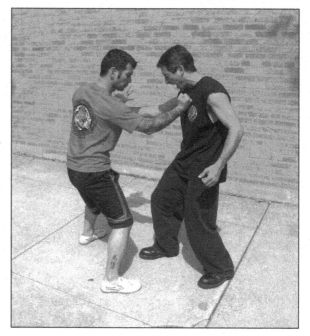

Tsai executes a hammer fist to the attacker's collar bone.

Tsai executes a back fist to the attacker's temple.

Technique J continued

Tsai delivers a forearm strike to the attacker's arm.

Tsai strikes his attacker
with a palm heel strike to the jaw.

Technique K

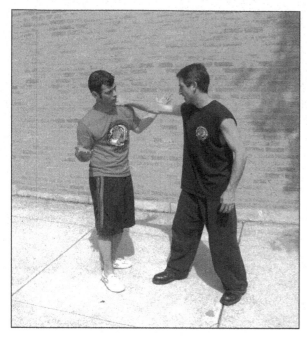

The attacker grabs Tsai's left shoulder.

Tsai delivers a palm strike to the attacker's chest.

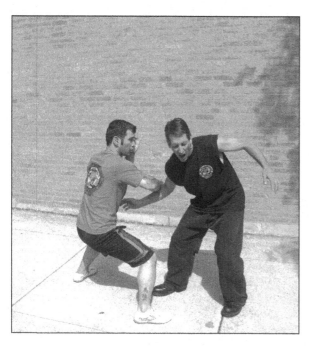

Tsai delivers a knife hand to the attacker's forearm.

Technique K continued

Tsai executes a knife hand to the attacker's neck.

Tsai roundhouse kicks the attacker in his support leg.

Technique L

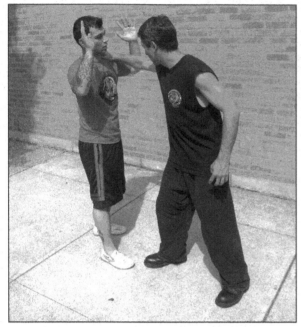

The attacker grabs Tsai's left shoulder.

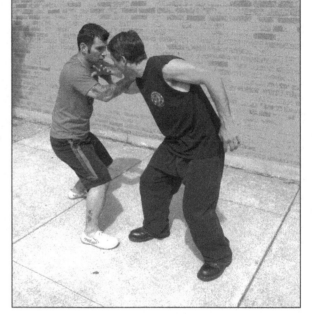

Tsai strikes attacker in the bend of the elbow.

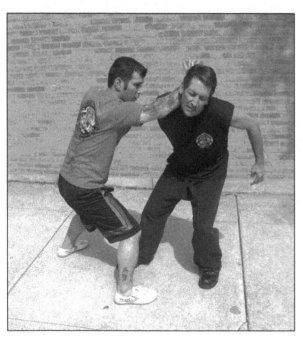

Tsai delivers a forearm strike to the attacker's neck.

Technique L continued

Tsai executes a roundhouse kick.

Technique M

The attacker grabs Tsai and prepares to deliver a strike.

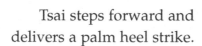

Tsai steps forward and delivers a palm heel strike.

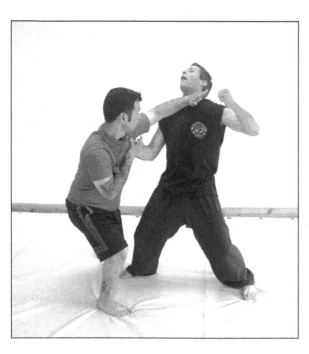

Tsai delivers a knife hand to the attacker's neck.

Technique M continued

Tsai strikes the attacker in the solar plexus.

Tsai interlocks his hands
around the attacker's neck.

Tsai delivers a knee strike to the attacker's midsection.

Technique N

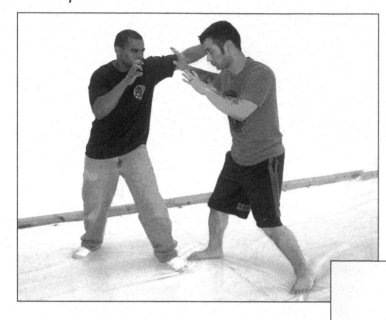

The attacker reaches to apply a headlock on Tsai.

The attacker has Tsai in a headlock.

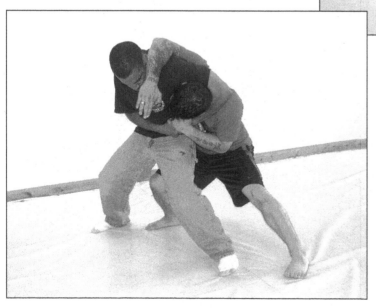

Tsai wraps his right arm around the attacker's head.

Technique N continued

Tsai pulls back on the attacker's head.

Tsai steps back and throws the attacker to the ground.

Technique O

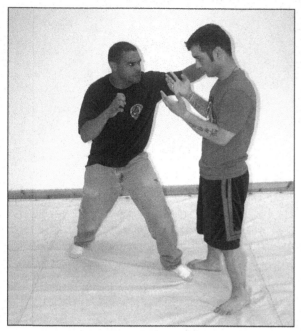

The attacker reaches to apply a headlock on Tsai.

The attacker has Tsai in a headlock.

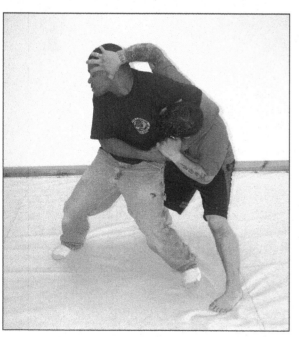

Tsai attacks a pressure point behind the ear in the attacker's neck.

Technique O continued

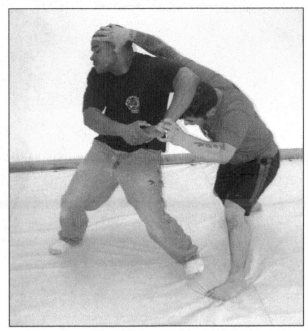

Tsai steps back and releases himself from the head lock.

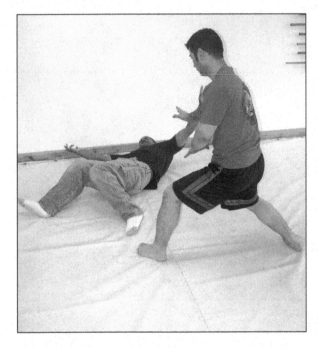

Tsai pulls the attacker down to the ground.

Technique P

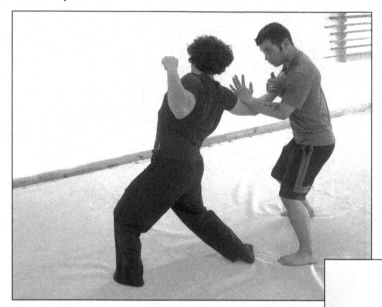

Tsai steps back and strikes the attacker in the bend of the elbow.

Tsai executes a palm strike to the attacker's ear.

Tsai applies a joint lock to the attacker's wrist.

Technique P continued

Tsai brings the attacker to the ground by applying pressure to the wrist lock.

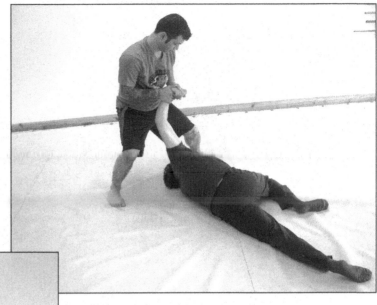

Tsai breaks the attacker's wrist.

Technique Q

The attacker grabs Tsai.

Tsai steps back and strikes the attacker in the bend of the elbow.

Tsai delivers a vertical punch to the attacker's face.

Technique Q continued

Tsai executes a palm strike
to the attacker's head.

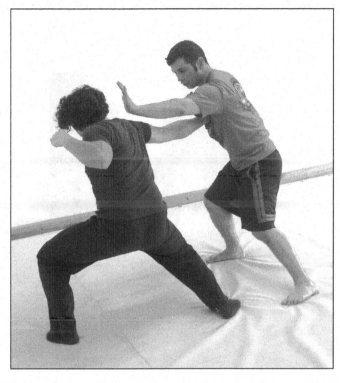

Tsai delivers a roundhouse
kick to the attacker's chest.

Technique R

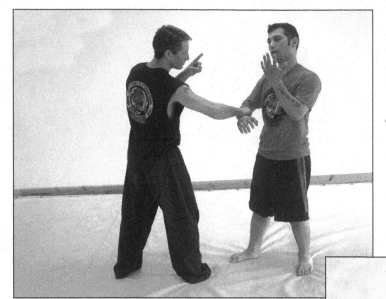

The attacker grabs Tsai.

Tsai places his left arm in the bend of the attacker's elbow.

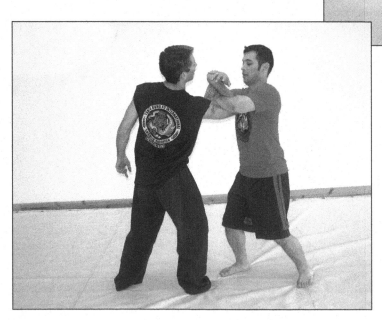

Tsai creates two circular movements with his arm creating a joint lock.

Technique R continued

Tsai forces the attacker to the ground by applying pressure to the wrist joint.

Technique S

The attacker grabs Tsai.

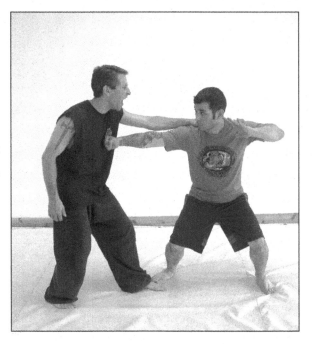

Tsai executes a back fist to the attacker's solar plexus.

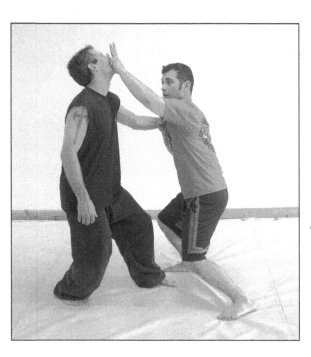

Tsai delivers a palm heel strike to the attacker's chin.

Technique S continued

Tsai executes a vertical punch to the attacker's floating ribs.

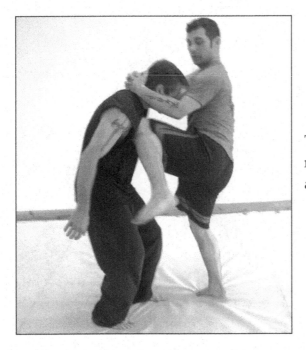

Tsai grabs the back of the attacker's neck while throwing a knee strike to the attacker's midsection.

Technique T

The attacker grabs Tsai around the throat.

Tsai drops his body weight.

Tsai executes a spear hand to the attacker's throat.

Technique T continued

Tsai delivers a palm heel
strike to the attacker's forehead.

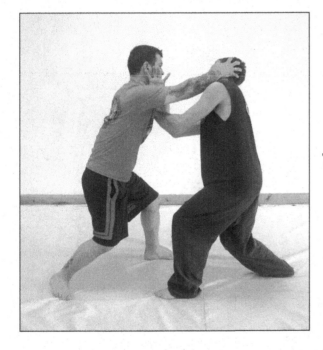

Tsai executes a palm strike to the attacker's ear.

Technique U

The attacker grabs Tsai.

Tsai strikes the attacker's neck
with the knife hand.

Tsai grabs the attacker around his neck.

Technique U continued

Thrusting his head, Tsai
throws the attacker to the ground.

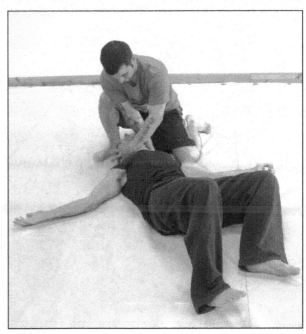

Technique V

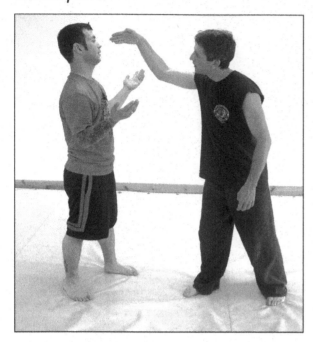

The attacker confronts Tsai.

Tsai pushes the attacker's arm to the inside.

Tsai executes a back fist to the attacker's nose.

Technique V continued

Tsai sweeps the lead leg of his attacker.

Tsai throws the attacker to the ground.

Technique W

The attacker grabs Tsai with both hands.

Tsai counters by striking to the neck.

Tsai executes a palm strike to the attacker's head.

Technique W continued

Tsai rotates forward and executes an elbow strike.

Tsai finishes the attacker off by
one last strike to the attacker's throat.

Chapter 9

Defense against a Bear Hug

A bear hug can be used as an initial assault or as a follow-through technique. In this chapter we will look at both a front and rear bear hug. Remaining calm and executing properly is key. This is where that strong foundation you built doing the basics really comes into play. This chapter will also reinforce your understanding of target areas. Striking or applying pressure to the appropriate target areas assists in setting up the assailant for the release from the bear hug.

Technique A

The attacker grabs Tsai into a bear hug.

Tsai steps back to create distance.

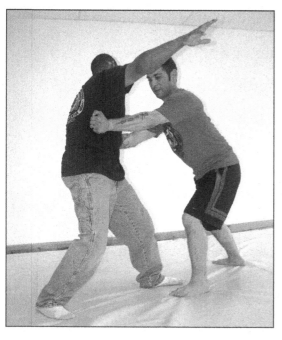

Tsai grabs the attacker on both sides of the attacker's abdomen to grab tendons and muscle around the rib cage.

Technique A continued

Tsai delivers a right-handed vertical punch to the attacker's solar plexus.

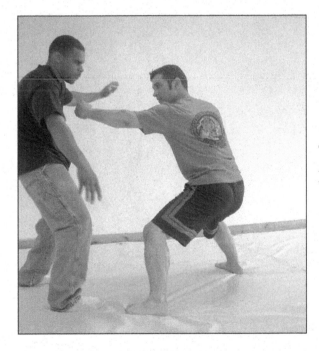

Tsai delivers a left-handed vertical punch to the attacker's solar plexus.

Technique B

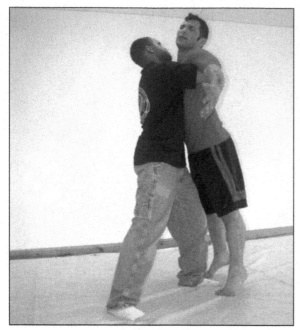

The attacker grabs Tsai into a bear hug.

Tsai double palm slaps his attacker's ear drum.

Tsai executes a head butt to the attacker.

Technique B continued

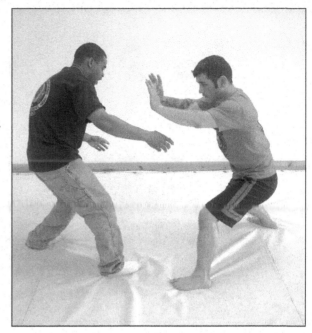

Tsai pushes the attacker away.

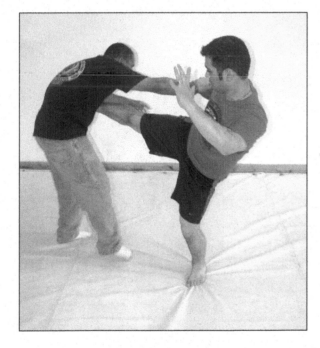

Tsai executes a roundhouse kick to the attacker.

Technique C

The attacker places Tsai into a full nelson.

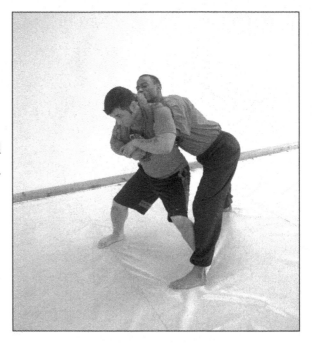

Tsai grabs the attacker's wrist and forces his arms and shoulders down.

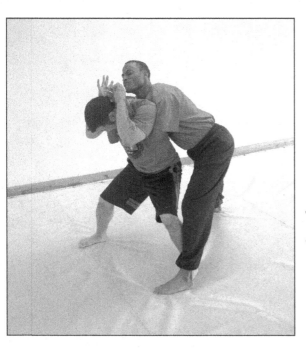

Tsai grabs the attacker's fingers and separates the attacker's hands.

Technique C continued

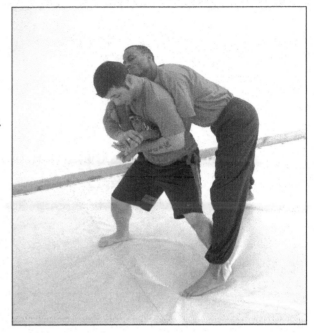

Tsai creates a wrist lock on the attacker.

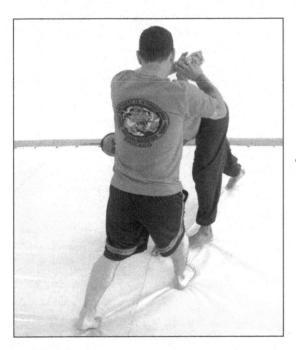

Tsai rotates to his left.

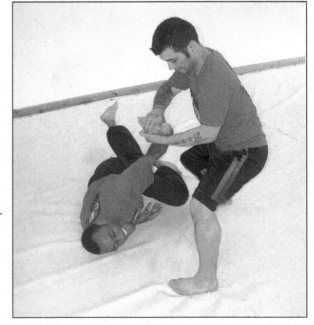

Tsai breaks the attacker's fingers.

Technique D

The attacker grabs Tsai under his arms in a bear hug.

Dropping into a horse stance, Tsai strikes the attacker's hands causing the attacker to let go.

Tsai rotates to his left, striking the attacker with an elbow to the temple.

Technique D continued

Stepping through to his left, Tsai executes a cutting palm technique to the attacker's jaw.

Tsai finishes off with a front snap kick to his solar plexus.

Technique E

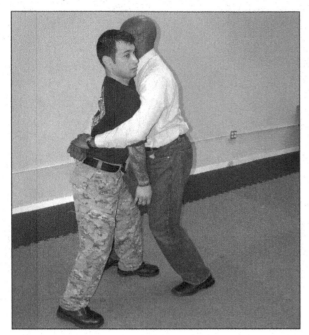

The attacker grabs Tsai around his arms in a bear hug.

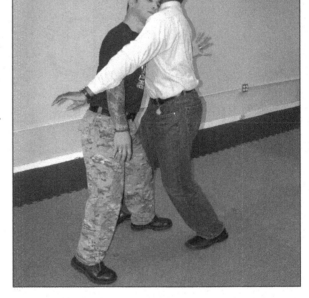

Tsai delivers a head butt to the attacker's head.

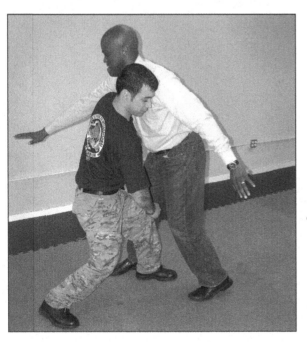

Tsai strikes the attacker in the groin.

Technique E continued

Tsai slides forward and delivers a reverse punch.

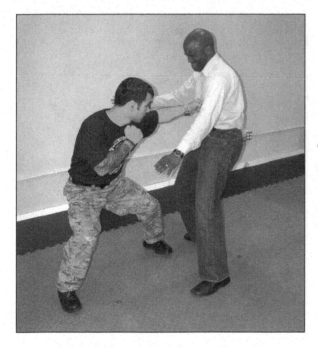

Tsai delivers a vertical punch to the attacker's solar plexus.

Technique F

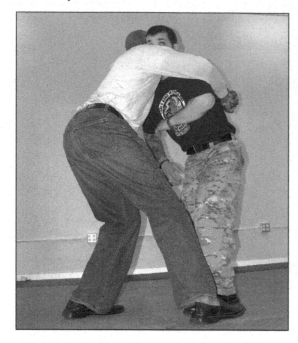

The attacker grabs Tsai around his arms in a bear hug. Tsai drops his body weight and pushes both elbows out to the side.

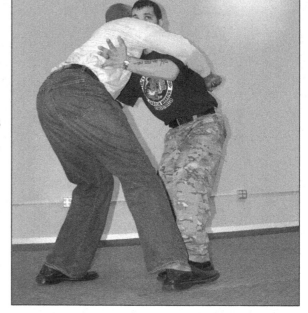

Tsai grabs the attacker with both arms and creates space between them.

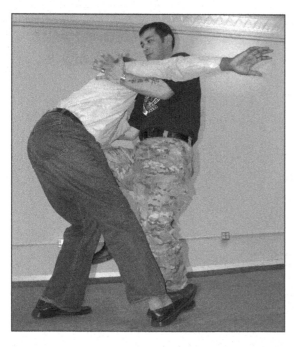

Tsai delivers a knee strike to the opponent's groin.

Technique F continued

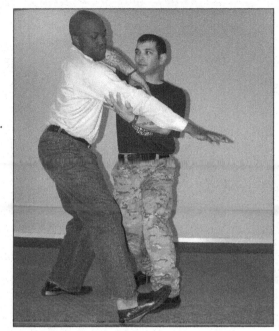

Tsai delivers an elbow strike to the attacker's neck.

Tsai executes a cutting punch to the attacker's midsection.

Technique G

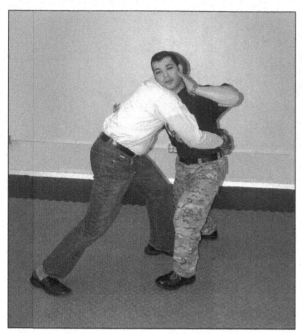

The attacker engages Tsai into a bear hug. Tsai slips his left arm loose.

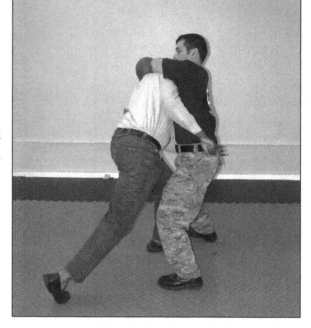

Tsai executes a palm heel strike to the attacker's ear.

Close-up of palm heel strike.

Technique G continued

Tsai throws a knee strike to the attacker.

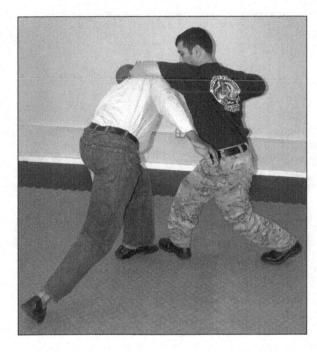

Tsai delivers an elbow strike to the attacker's jaw.

Technique H

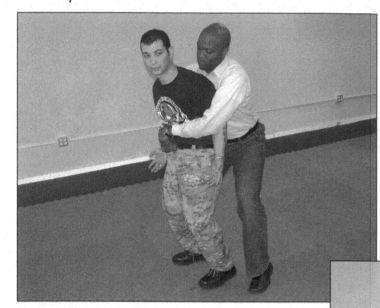

The attacker engages Tsai into a bear hug from behind.

Tsai drops his body weight and pushes his arms out to the side.

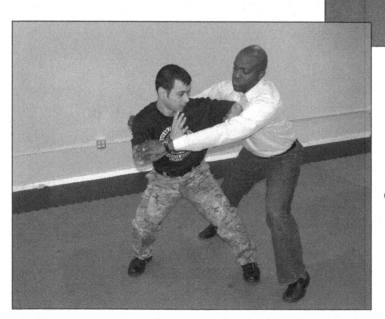

Tsai rotates toward the attacker and delivers an elbow strike to the sternum.

Technique H continued

Tsai continues rotating while executing a back fist to the face.

Tsai finishes the attacker with a reverse punch to the neck.

Technique 1

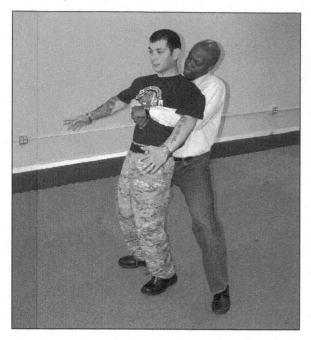

The attacker engages Tsai into a bear hug from behind.

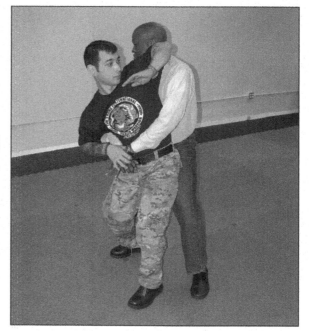

Tsai rotates toward the attacker and delivers an elbow strike to the head.

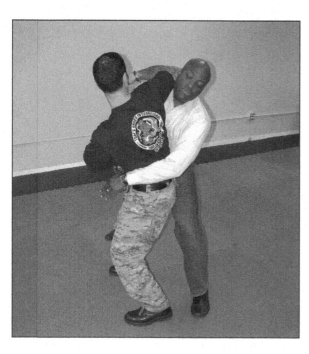

Tsai rotates to the other side and delivers an elbow strike to the head.

Technique I continued

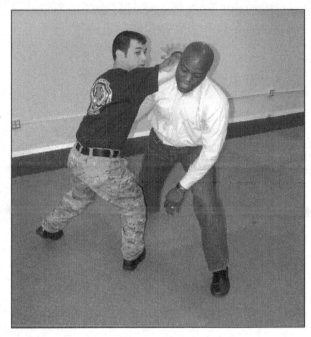

Tsai continues rotating to the right, escaping from the bear hug.

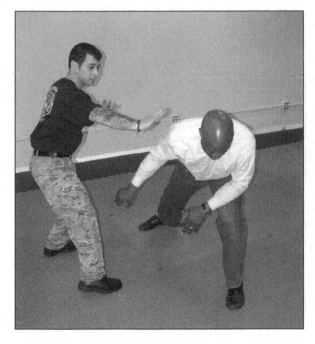

Tsai is released from the bear hug as the attacker falls to the ground.

Technique J

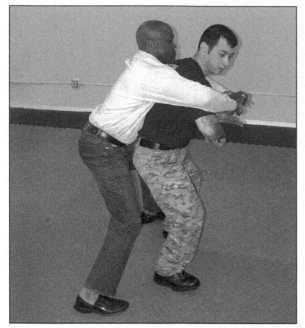

The attacker engages Tsai into a bear hug from behind.

Tsai places his hands inside of the grab and uses his body weight and arm strength to break the grab.

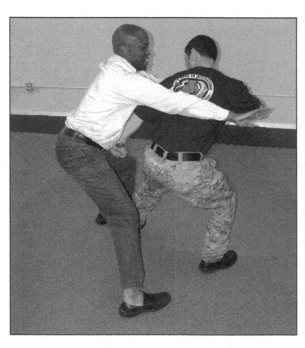

Tsai rotates to his left and delivers a hammer fist to the groin.

Technique J continued

Tsai ducks under the attacker's right arm.

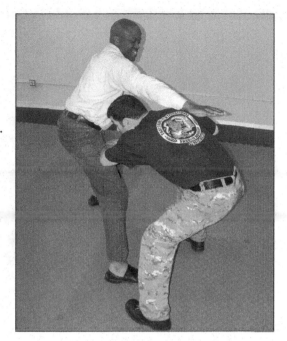

Tsai delivers a cutting punch
to the opponent's floating ribs.

Technique K

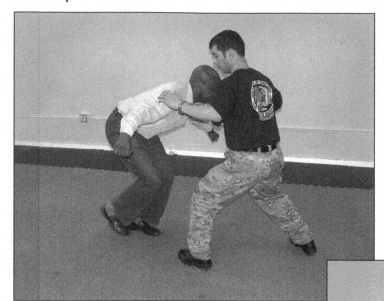

The attacker rushes in to grab Tsai.

Tsai is caught in the bear hug.

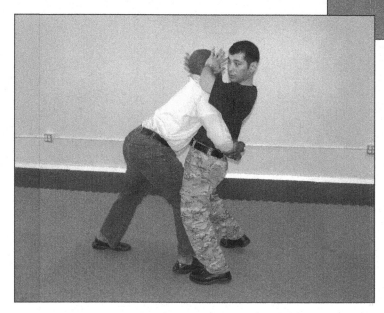

Tsai delivers a palm heel strike to the attacker's head.

Technique K continued

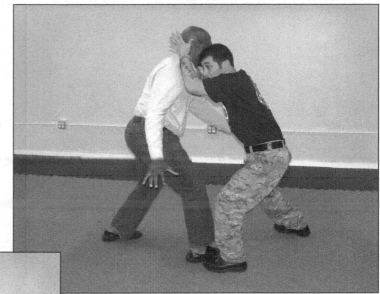

Tsai head butts the attacker.

Tsai delivers a knee to the attacker's groin.

Chapter 10

Defense against a Shove

Often an attacker will use a shove as an opener and means to blindside his victim. If you are unsuspecting, the shove is a good way to knock you off balance and disorient you while your assailant follows through with the attack.

In this chapter, we will to show you how to regain your footing and balance immediately and use the initial momentum of the shove to your advantage.

Technique A

The opponent attempts to shove Tsai.

Tsai rotates to the outside allowing the opponent to go by.

Tsai delivers a palm strike to the opponent's face.

Technique A continued

Tsai reaches for the opponent's shoulders.

Tsai delivers a knee strike to the opponent.

Technique B

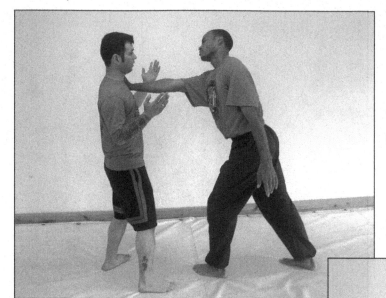

The attacker shoves Tsai on his left shoulder.

Tsai rotates to his left while delivering a strike with his right hand.

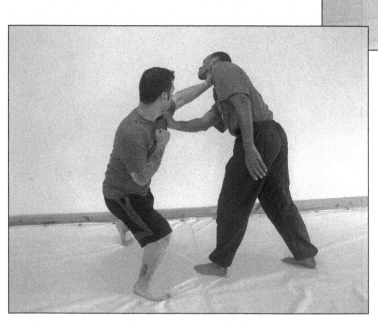

Tsai executes a knife hand to the attacker's neck.

Technique B continued

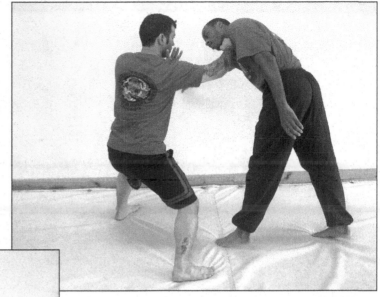

Tsai delivers a vertical punch to the attacker's neck.

Tsai executes a knee strike to the attacker's chest.

Technique C

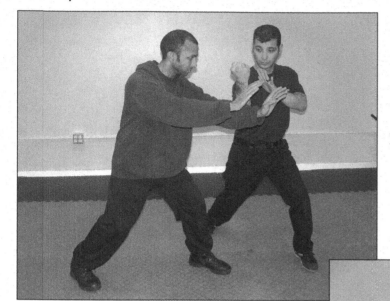

The attacker attempts to shove Tsai while he deflects the attempt using his forearm.

Tsai counters with a back fist to the opponent's jaw.

Tsai delivers a side kick to the opponent's knee.

Technique C continued

Tsai prepares to execute another side kick.

Tsai stomps on the attacker's ankle.

Technique D

The attacker attempts to shove Tsai while he deflects the attempt.

Tsai counters by preparing to execute a front snap kick.

Tsai delivers a front snap kick to the solar plexus.

Technique D continued

Tsai steps down after the kick.

Tsai throws a reverse punch to the opponent's neck.

Technique E

The attacker attempts to shove Tsai.

Tsai counters by deflecting the pushing hand downward.

Tsai grabs the attacker's arm while delivering a knife hand to the neck.

Technique E continued

Tsai executes a knee strike.

Tsai steps down and delivers a vertical punch to the jaw.

Technique F

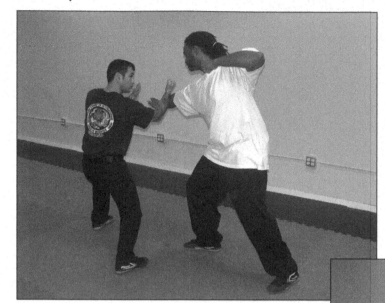

The opponent attempts to push Tsai as he deflects the arm to the outside.

Tsai steps forward and delivers a back fist to the jaw of the opponent.

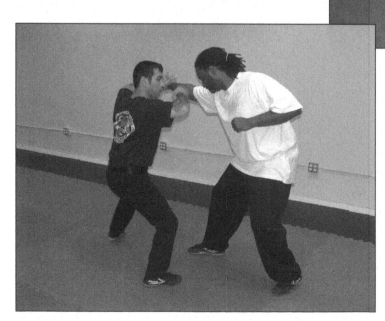

Tsai rechambers his striking arm.

Technique F continued

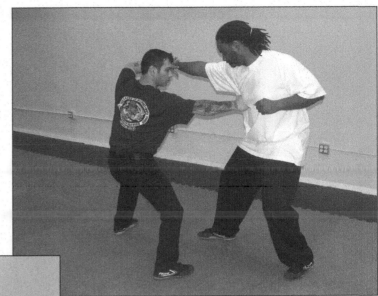

Tsai delivers a back fist strike to the midsection.

Tsai finishes the opponent by delivering a front snap kick.

Technique G

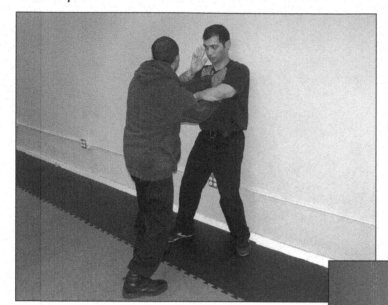

Tsai is pushed against a wall.

Tsai rotates to the outside and deflects the shove.

Tsai grabs the attacker's arm with his left hand while striking the neck with his right arm.

Technique G continued

Tsai prepares to strike the opponent.

Tsai strikes the back
of the opponent's elbow.

Technique H

Tsai is shoved against the wall.

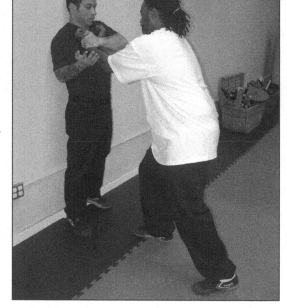

Tsai traps the opponent's arms with his left arm.

Tsai delivers a palm heel strike to the opponent's nose.

Technique H continued

Tsai punches the opponent's throat.

Tsai finishes the attacker by delivering a roundhouse kick to the groin.

Technique 1

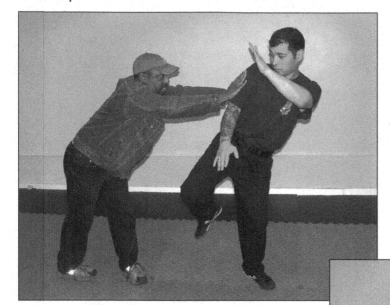

Tsai is pushed by the attacker.

Catching his balance,
Tsai cross steps backward.

Tsai stops his backward momentum by
planting his feet and dropping into
a fighting stance.

Technique I continued

Tsai moves forward into his opponent.

Tsai delivers a side kick into the opponent's solar plexus.

Technique J

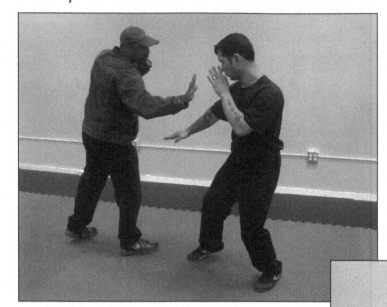

The attacker moves forward with a right shave.

Tsai counters the push by blocking with a cross block.

Tsai delivers a cutting punch to the attacker's floating ribs.

Technique J continued

Tsai strikes the attacker in the head with a palm strike.

Tsai finishes the attacker with a front snap kick to the face.

Technique K

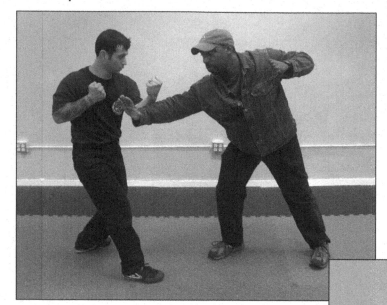

The attacker attempts to push Tsai and Tsai counters the push by blocking with a left cross block.

Tsai delivers a reverse punch to the attacker's jaw.

Tsai kicks the attacker with a front snap kick.

Technique K continued

The attacker falls to the ground as a result of the front snap kick.

Tsai delivers a reverse punch to the opponent's head.

Technique L

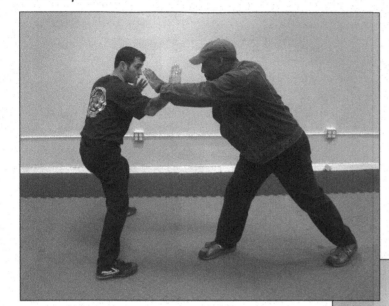

The attacker attempts to push Tsai.

Tsai blocks the attacker's advance utilizing an upward block.

Tsai delivers a cutting punch to the attacker's ribs.

Technique L continued

Tsai executes a roundhouse kick.

The attacker falls to the ground as a result of the roundhouse kick.

Technique M

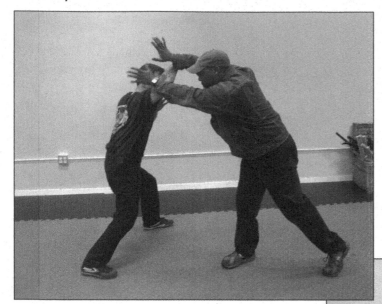

Tsai blocks the attacker's advance utilizing an upward block.

Tsai steps to the outside and delivers a front kick to the groin.

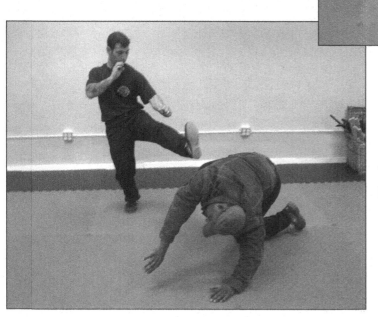

Tsai delivers an additional front kick to knock the attacker to the ground.

Technique M continued

Tsai steps down and prepares to attack again.

Tsai executes a finishing front kick to the opponent's floating ribs.

Chapter 11

Defense against a Knife

It is becoming increasingly common for people to be armed.
Knives are often carried because many are legal to buy, are
easily concealed, and are easy to learn to use.

It is important not to get fixated on the knife if it is used in an
attack. You still must block and stop the attacking arm along
with the attacking person. There are ways to turn the knife on
your attacker while keeping yourself in one piece. Striking
power becomes even more important because expediency is key
to stopping a knife attack. The longer the attack goes on the
better your chance of being cut, so you must execute with force.

We'll show you how to stop the knife attack right away, disable
the attacker, and give yourself the "edge."

Technique A

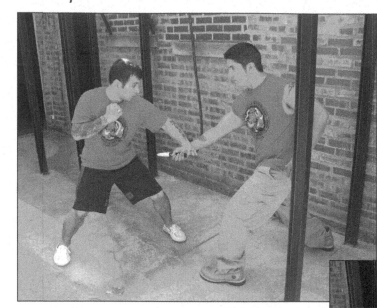

The attacker attempts to stab Tsai with a knife. Tsai executes a downward block.

Tsai delivers a hammer fist to the attacker's biceps.

Tsai delivers a back fist to the temple of the attacker.

Technique A continued

Tsai delivers a roundhouse
kick to the attacker's groin.

Tsai steps down and throws a reverse
punch to the attacker's jaw.

Technique B

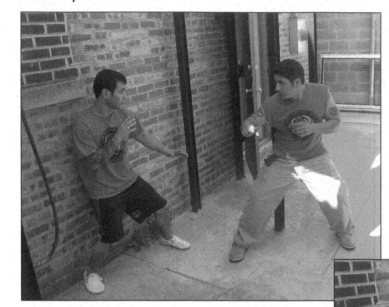

Tsai is backed into a wall
by an attacker with a knife.

The attacker stabs at Tsai while he blocks
the attack to the inside with both hands.

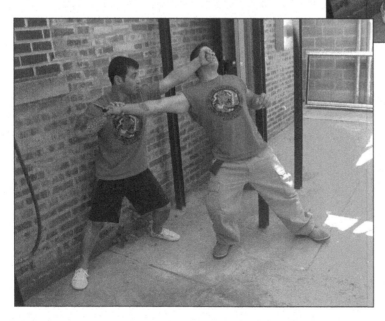

Tsai secures the knife with one hand and
executes a back fist with his left hand.

Technique B continued

Tsai bends the attacker's wrist
and slams him into the wall.

Tsai delivers a vertical
punch to the neck of the opponent.

Technique C

The attacker, armed with a knife, engages Tsai.

Tsai blocks the attacker's stab and strikes the biceps of the attacker.

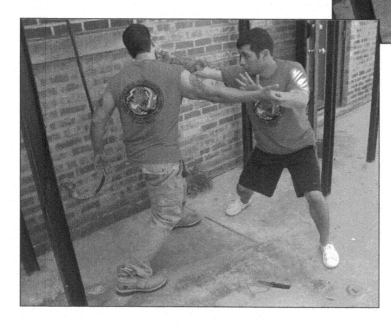

Tsai delivers a vertical punch to the attacker's jaw.

Technique C continued

Tsai throws a roundhouse
kick to the attacker's back.

Technique D

The attacker slices the knife toward Tsai.

Tsai strikes the attacker's elbow, causing him to release the knife.

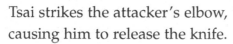

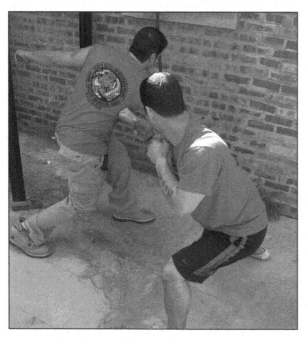

Tsai throws a cutting punch to the attacker's floating ribs.

Technique D continued

Tsai throws a front snap kick to the attacker's floating ribs.

Technique E

The attacker attempts to stab Tsai in the chest with the knife. Tsai executes an inside block.

Tsai strikes the attacker's lead leg with a front snap kick.

Tsai controls the attacker's arm with the knife.

Technique E continued

Tsai pulls the attacker forward to extend the arm and attack the elbow.

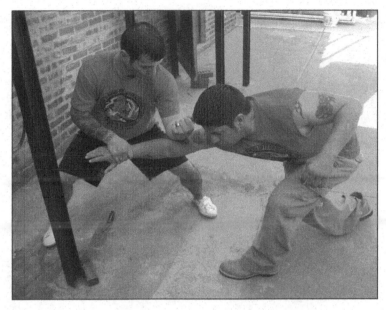

Technique F

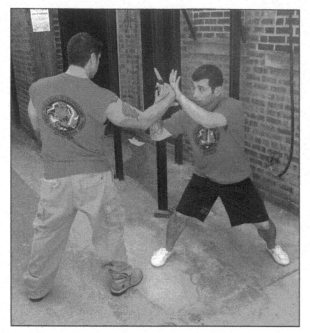

The attacker attempts to stab Tsai with the knife. Tsai grabs the attacker's wrist and fights for control.

Tsai executes a front snap kick to the attacker.

Tsai steps forward and strikes the attacker in the neck with a knife hand strike.

Technique F continued

Tsai reaches around the attacker's neck and pulls him off balance.

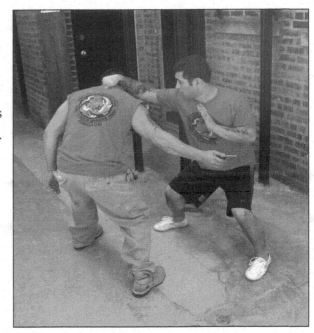

Tsai rotates the attacker's head into a pole in the alley.

Technique G

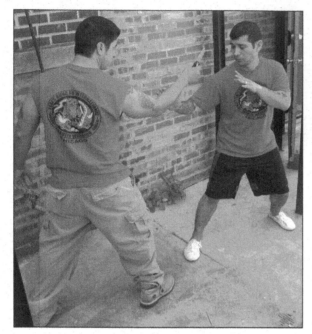

The attacker confronts Tsai with a knife.

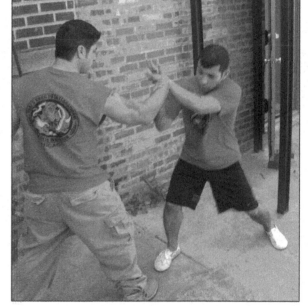

Tsai fights for control of the knife.

Tsai executes a front snap kick to the attacker.

Technique G continued

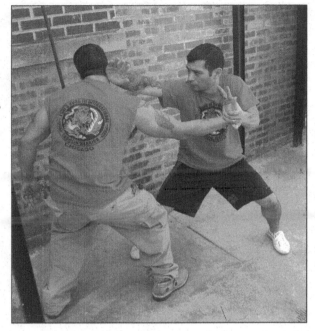

Tsai steps forward and strikes the attacker in the neck with a knife hand strike.

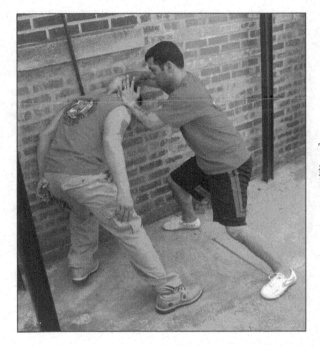

Tsai slams the attacker's head into the brick wall of the building.

Technique H

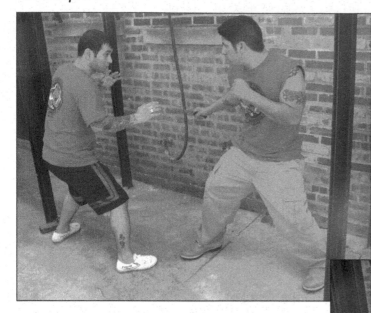

The attacker confronts Tsai with a knife.

The attacker attempts to stab Tsai. Tsai blocks the striking arm by punching the attacker's bicep.

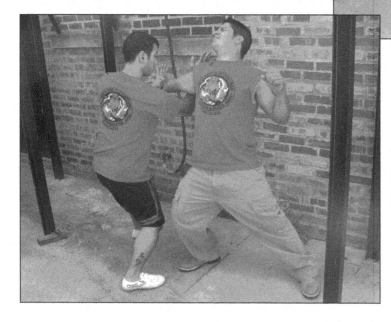

Tsai controls the attacker's wrist with his left hand, slipping his arm under and propping the elbow with his right arm.

Technique H continued

Tsai steps behind the attacker's lead leg
and prepares to strike the attacker.

Tsai finishes the attacker with a palm strike
to the head, which drives the attacker's
head into the brick wall.

Technique 1

The attacker lunges at Tsai with a knife. Tsai deflects the knife to the inside using his lead arm.

Using his right arm, Tsai guides the knife to the outside.

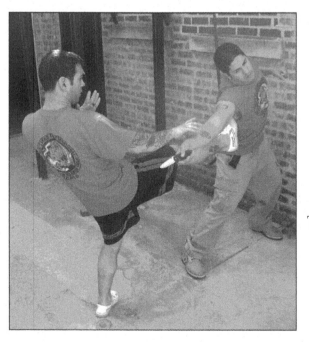

Tsai executes a front snap kick to the attacker.

Technique I continued

Tsai grabs the attacker's wrist, and strikes his elbow, causing the attacker to release the knife.

Tsai finishes by executing a cutting punch to the base of the attacker's skull.

Technique J

The attacker slashes at Tsai's head. Tsai ducks under the slashing arm to avoid the knife.

Tsai counters with a hook punch to the attacker's floating ribs.

Tsai rotates to his left and delivers a hook punch to the body.

Technique J continued

Tsai grabs the attacker's wrist.

Tsai locks the attacker's wrist
and rotates the attacker to the ground.

Technique K

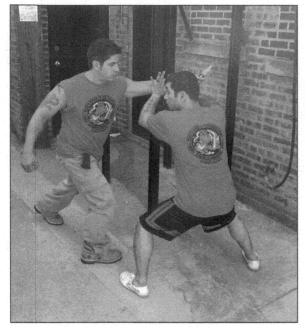

The attacker attempts to stab Tsai in the head. Tsai sidesteps and blocks the attack.

Tsai slams the attacker's arm into the metal pole.

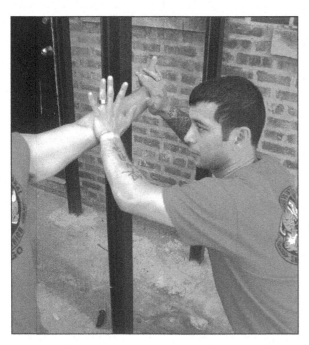

Close-up.

Technique K continued

Tsai delivers a hook punch to the solar plexus.

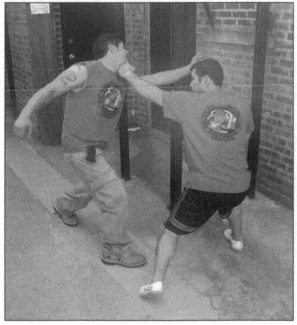

Tsai delivers a cutting punch to the jaw.

Tsai finishes the attacker
with a roundhouse kick to the ribs.

Technique L

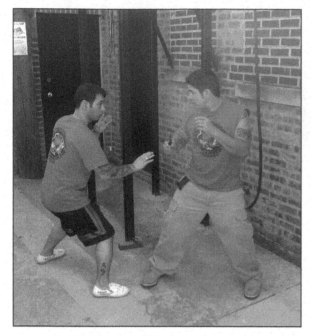

Tsai and attacker square off in an alley.

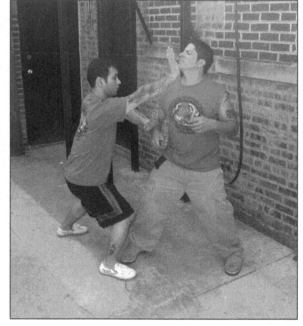

Tsai lunges forward to jam the attacker. Tsai executes a palm heel strike to the jaw while controlling the arm with the knife.

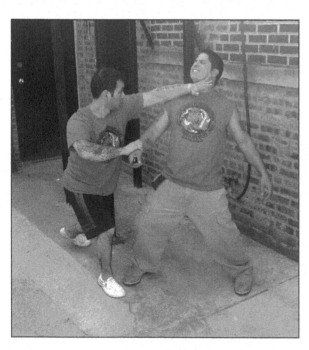

Tsai grabs the arm with the knife and strikes the neck of the attacker.

Technique L continued

Tsai sweeps the lead leg of the attacker.

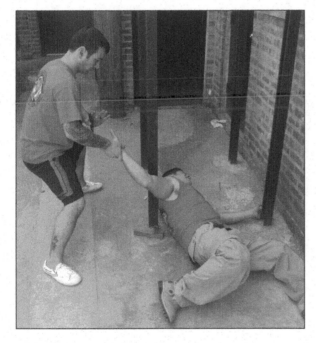

The attacker falls to the ground as a result of the sweep. Tsai remains in control of the arm with the knife.

Chapter 12

Defense against a Surprise Attack

You've heard it enough. Stay alert. Stay alert. Stay alert.
The fact is, even though we have the best of intentions, our
minds do wander from time to time. Violent people
look for these opportunities, and it can be argued that
the majority of attacks are surprise attacks.

This chapter takes that into account and will teach you
how to use the element of surprise to your own advantage
and turn the tables on your unsuspecting assailant.

Technique A

Tsai is standing on the street when the would-be attacker walks up.

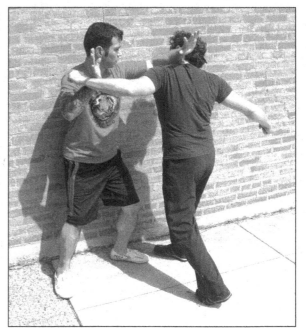

The attacker swings with his left arm. Tsai blocks with his right arm and delivers a forearm strike with his left arm.

Tsai pushes the attacker's head into the brick wall.

Technique A continued

Tsai executes a right knee strike to the attacker's face.

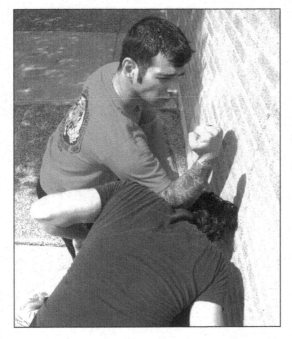

Tsai delivers an elbow strike to the attacker's neck.

Technique B

The attacker pushes Tsai against the car. Tsai pushes the attacker's arms together.

Tsai's left palm grabs the attacker's neck, and he palm strikes the attacker's jaw.

Tsai executes an elbow strike to the attacker's jaw.

Technique B continued

Tsai rotates the attacker's head and body around to the right, slamming him into the car.

Technique C

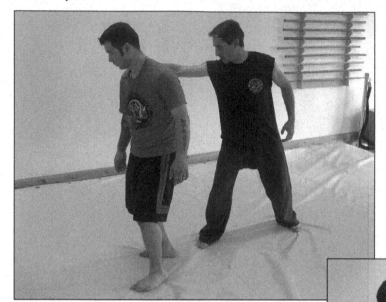

The attacker grabs Tsai's right shoulder.

Tsai grabs the attacker's hand and rotates to his right. Tsai delivers a side kick to the attacker's right knee joint.

Tsai strikes the attacker's elbow with a palm heel strike.

Technique C continued

Tsai executes a roundhouse kick to the attacker's thigh.

Tsai executes a knee strike to the attacker's floating ribs.

Technique D

The attacker grabs Tsai as he puts his keys in the door.

The attacker attempts to punch Tsai. Tsai executes an high block with his lead arm.

Tsai throws a vertical punch to the attacker's sternum.

Technique D continued

Tsai delivers a knee to the body.

Tsai finishes the attacker with a reverse punch to the floating ribs.

Technique E

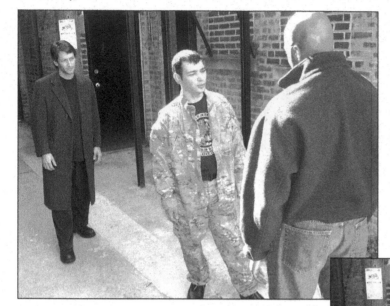

The attacker walks up while Tsai talks with another gentleman.

The attacker grabs Tsai from behind.

Tsai rotates to his right and delivers a palm strike with his right hand.

Technique E continued

Tsai executes a hammer fist strike to the attacker's jaw.

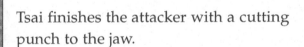

Tsai finishes the attacker with a cutting punch to the jaw.

Technique F

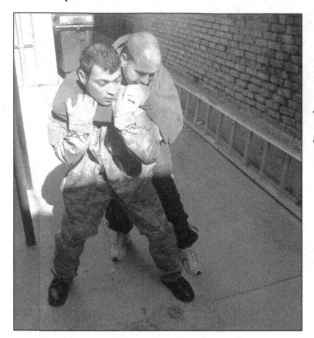

The attacker grabs Tsai from behind and places him in a choke hold.

Tsai drops his body weight and rotates to the inside.

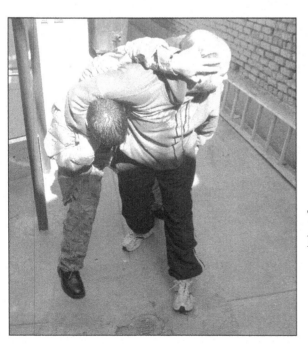

Tsai reaches to the back of the attacker's head and presses a pressure point behind the ear.

Technique F continued

Tsai is released and moves behind the attacker.

Tsai punches the attacker
in the kidneys.

Technique G

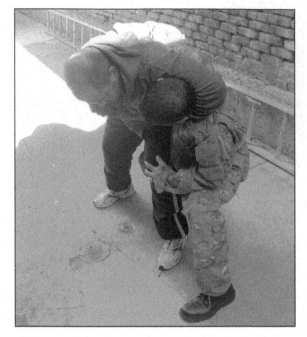

Tsai is grabbed from the side by the attacker.

Tsai places his right forearm on the side of the attacker's head, and places his knife hand under the attacker's nose.

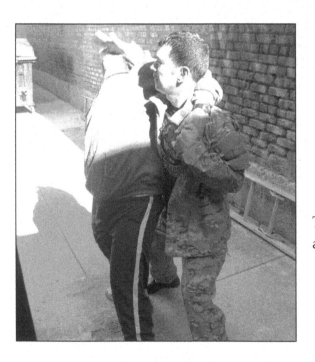

Tsai pushes with his right hand against the attacker's head driving the nose back.

Technique G continued

Tsai extends his right arm and removes the attacker's left arm from around his neck.

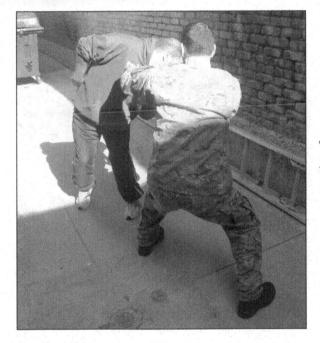

Tsai steps forward and delivers a vertical punch to the attacker's jaw.

Technique H

The attacker grabs Tsai and places him in a headlock.

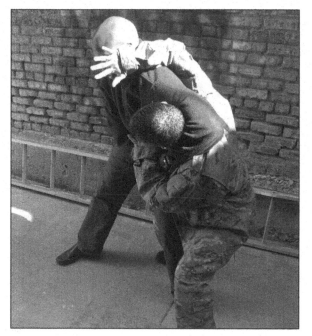

Tsai pushes against the attacker's head with his right hand and pulls down against his attacker's left hand.

Tsai strikes his attacker's groin.

Technique H continued

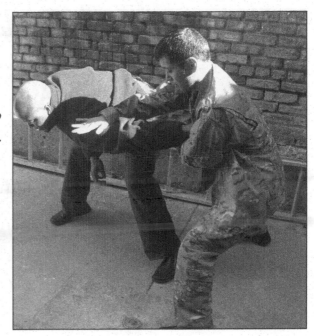

Tsai rolls out of his attacker's grip and places his arm in a joint lock.

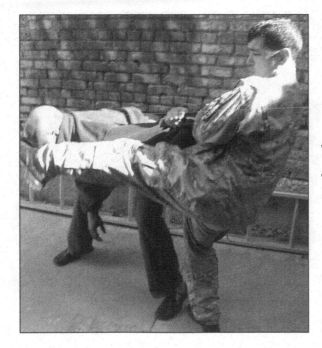

Tsai finishes the attacker with a front snap kick to the face.

Technique 1

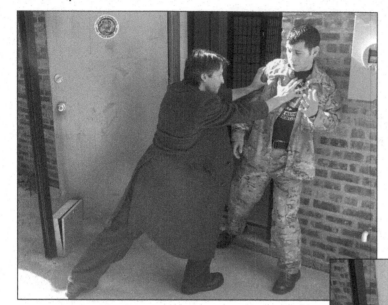

Tsai walks out the door and is immediately pushed against the wall.

The attacker throws a reverse punch and Tsai defends with his right arm.

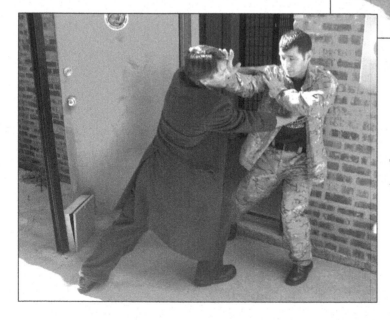

Tsai palm strikes the attacker with his right arm.

Technique I continued

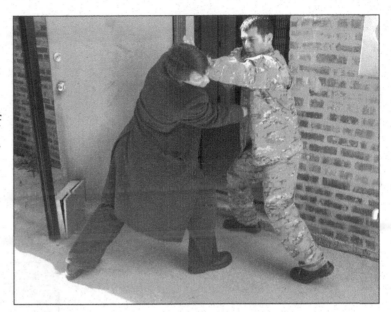

Tsai finishes the attacker off with a knife hand to his neck.

Technique J

Tsai walks out the door and is immediately pushed against the wall.

Tsai palm strikes the attacker with his right arm.

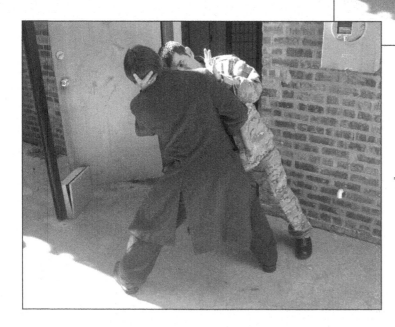

Tsai executes a head butt to the attacker.

Technique J continued

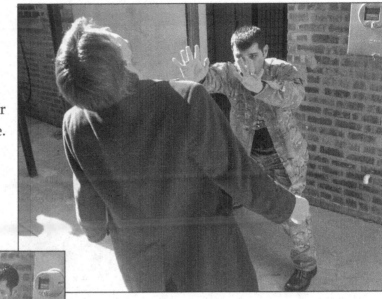

Tsai pushes the attacker back to create space.

Tsai finishes the attacker with a roundhouse kick to the stomach area.

Technique K

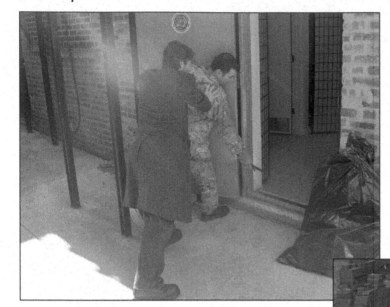

Tsai is attacked from behind. The attacker shoves Tsai into a door.

Tsai prepares to execute a back kick into the attacker.

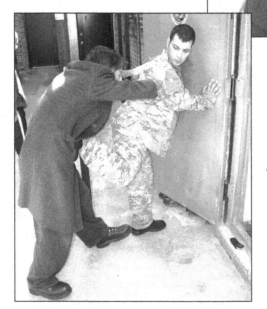

Tsai back kicks the attacker in his stomach.

Technique K continued

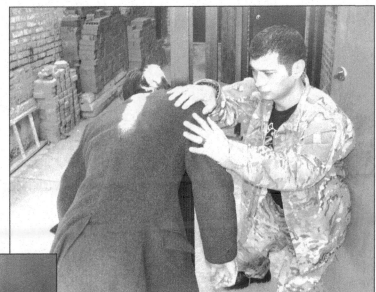

Using his surroundings, Tsai rams the attacker's head into a pole.

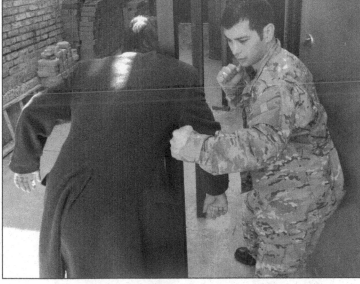

Tsai finishes with a hook punch to the floating ribs.

Technique L

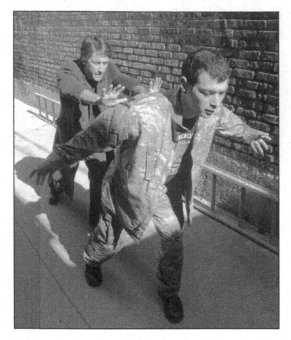

The attacker shoves Tsai in the back, and Tsai stumbles forward.

Tsai rotates to his right and executes a side kick to the attacker's midsection.

Tsai steps down and throws a back fist to the attacker's face.

Technique L continued

Tsai delivers a reverse punch to the solar plexus.

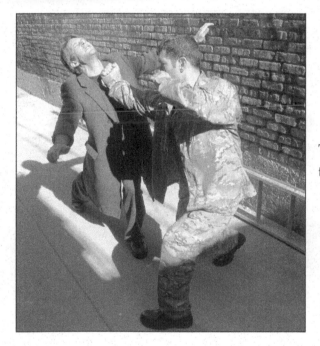

Tsai finishes the attacker with an uppercut to the attacker's jaw.

Technique M

Tsai is confronted by an attacker while he is seated in a chair.

Tsai grabs the attacker's hand with his left hand while bending his finger back with his right hand.

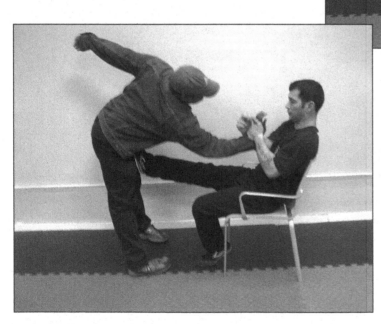

Tsai executes a front snap kick to the groin.

Technique M continued

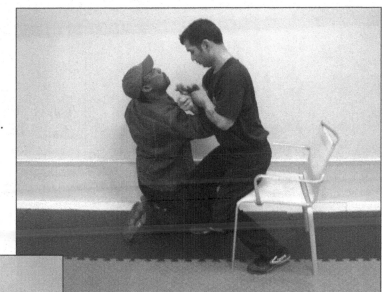

Tsai brings the attacker down to his knees.

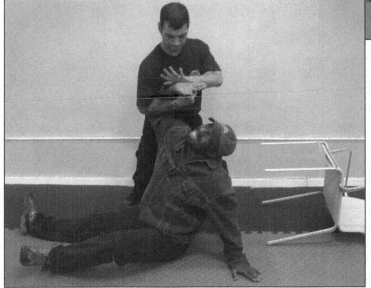

Tsai finishes the attacker by breaking the attacker's finger.

Technique N

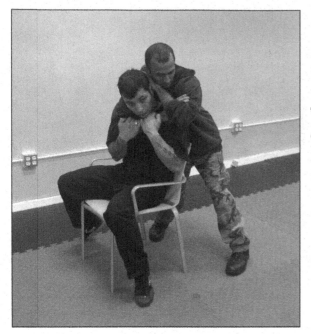

Tsai is put in a headlock from behind while sitting in a chair.

Tsai delivers an elbow strike to his attacker.

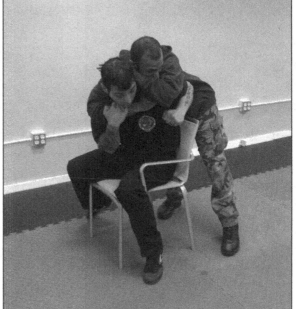

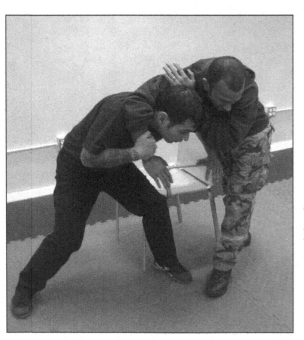

Tsai fights to his feet and begins to slip out of the headlock.

Technique N continued

Tsai slips out of the headlock.

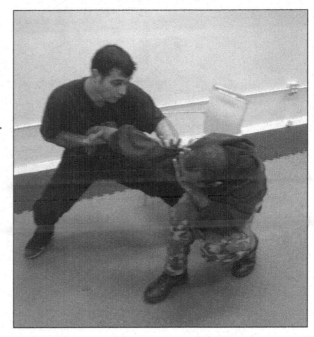

Tsai finishes the attacker with a knee strike to the ribs.

Technique O

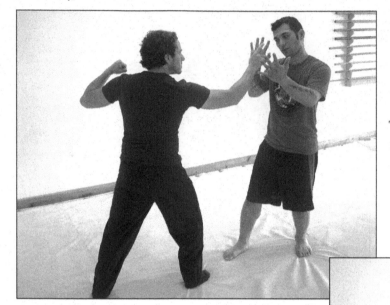

The attacker confronts Tsai.

Tsai grabs the attacker's wrist and braces his index finger.

Tsai bends the attacker's index finger back.

Technique O continued

Tsai takes his attacker to the ground using the index finger.

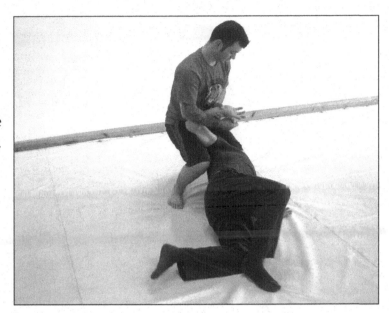

Chapter 13

Defense against Multiple Attackers

Often people attack in groups. The pack mentality is present in many living beings, and humans are no different. If you find yourself besieged by this kind of attack, you must use technique combined with strategy to be effective.

It is of the utmost importance to know how to leverage the additional people against each other instead of letting them get the advantage. You want them do the bulk of the work in your defense. You must turn the rhythm of the attack around in your favor.

This chapter presents defenses that will help you do just that. Please note, the exercises in this chapter contain more than five steps.

Technique A

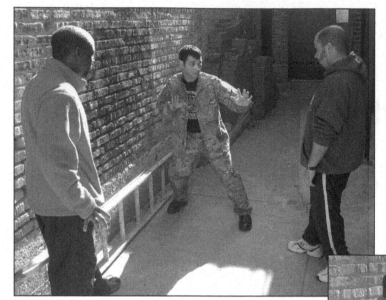

Tsai is confront by two attackers.

Attacker #1 throws a lunge punch at Tsai.

Tsai throws a reverse punch at the attacker, knocking the attacker back.

Technique A continued

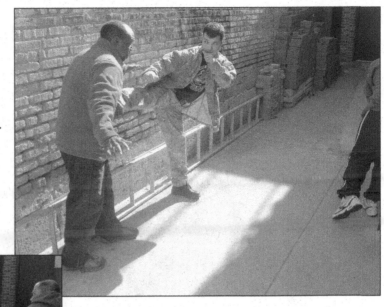

Tsai kicks attacker #2 in the midsection.

Tsai steps forward and hits attacker #2 with a back fist.

Tsai follows the vertical punch with a reverse punch to the body of attacker #2.

Technique A continued

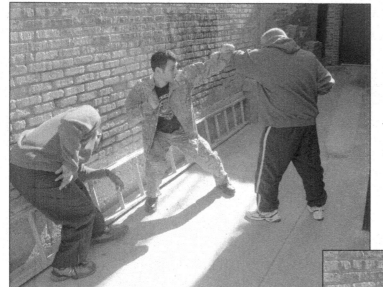

Attacker #1 throws a jab at Tsai.

Tsai counters with a reverse punch to the floating ribs.

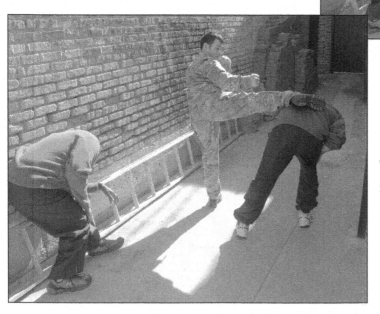

Tsai finishes the attacker with a roundhouse kick to the back.

Technique B

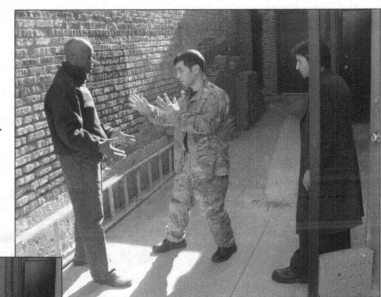

Tsai is attacked by two attackers.

Tsai hits attacker #1 with a
palm heel strike to the jaw.

Attacker #2 closes in with
a strike of his own.

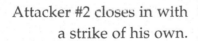

Technique B continued

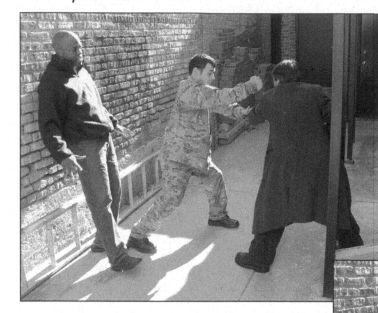

Tsai blocks and counters with a back fist to the face of attacker #2.

Tsai throws a side kick into attacker #1.

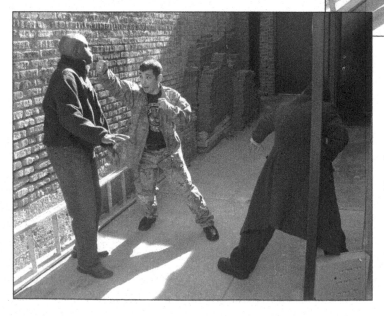

Tsai follows the side kick with a quick back fist to the attacker's jaw.

Technique B continued

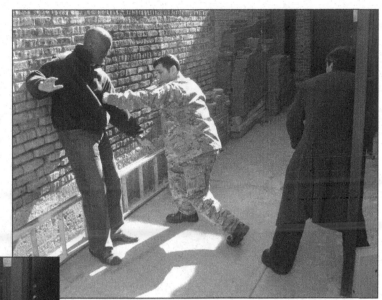

Following the back fist is a reverse punch to the attacker's midsection.

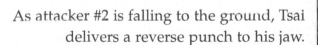

Tsai turns to his left and delivers a roundhouse kick to attacker #2.

As attacker #2 is falling to the ground, Tsai delivers a reverse punch to his jaw.

Technique C

Tsai is grabbed from behind and attacked by two additional attackers.

Tsai executes a front snap kick to attacker #2.

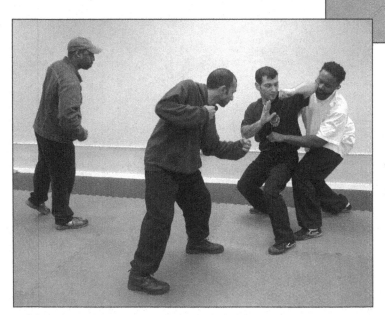

Tsai delivers an elbow strike to the jaw of attacker #1.

Technique C continued

Tsai executes a reverse
punch to attacker #2's jaw.

Tsai ducks under attacker #3's hook punch.

Tsai retaliates with a
hook punch to the body.

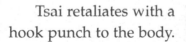

Technique C continued

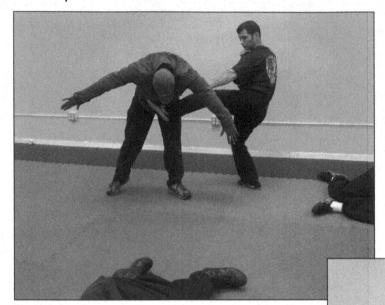

Tsai follows the hook punch with a roundhouse kick to the midsection.

Tsai finishes the attack with a front thrust kick to the back of attacker #3's head.

About the Authors

Waysun Johnny Tsai

Waysun Johnny Tsai was born in Chicago. He began his martial arts career at the age of eight under his father, Grandmaster John Chi Yuan Tsai. During this time he trained at the "Sheridan school" his father had established on the northside of Chicago. As he developed a certain proficiency in the arts, he concurrently began studying Tai Kit Kuen under the late Grandmaster Steven G. Abbate. Master Johnny began teaching children's classes at the young age of 14. When he was 16, Master Johnny received his 1st level black sash certification in both the Tsai Family Shaolin Fa Kung Fu system and Tai Kit Kung Fu system.

Today, Master Johnny is the chief U.S. representative for the Tsai Family Shaolin Chuan Fa Kung Fu system. He currently holds an eight degree black sash in both the Tsai Family system and the Tai Kit Kuen system. He has also served as an USAWKF full contact San Shou committee member. He has been featured on the cover of several international publications, such as Inside Kung Fu magazine and Art of the Warrior magazine. He has authored two combat Kung Fu DVDs. He owns and operates his own school in the southern suburbs of Chicago and serves as the curriculum advisor to 5 other Tsai Family Shaolin Fa system's certified schools.

He currently resides in Evergreen Park, Illinois, where he is constantly humbled by his greatest teachers: his wife Marlo and two children, Noah and Nyah.

For more information about Master Waysun Johnny Tsai, Shaolin Chuan Fa, or practical Kung Fu self defense seminars, please go to www.tsaiskungfu.net

Sifu Paula Lazarz

Sifu Paula Lazarz, a third-degree black sash, has been practicing Shaolin Kung Fu since 1992. She received her black sash within the Shaolin Chuan Fa system established in Chicago by renowned Grandmaster John Chi-Yuan Tsai. She has competed both locally and nationally and was a National Black Belt League (NBL) regional forms champion in 2003.

Currently, she owns and operates HealthKick Kung Fu and Energy Fitness Active Arts Center, both located in Chicago, Illinois.

Sifu Paula started training in Kung Fu for practical self-defense. Over her years of training she has developed a true passion and respect for the vast body of knowledge available in the art, not only for self-defense, but also for physical fitness and peace of mind.

She extends her gratitude to the Tsai family for introducing this amazing martial art to her and for their continued instruction and guidance.

Oren Headen

Over a span of two decades, Oren Headen (Sa Bum Nym, Chief Instructor) has diligently and relentlessly endured the training, hardships, and dedication required to excel in the martial arts. As a youth, Sa Bum Nym was introduced to the martial arts by his parents, Philip and Nadine Headen, who enrolled him in Shuri Ryu martial arts classes. After relocating to the south side of Chicago, Sa Bum Nym spent the next 17 years devoted to studying the art of Kuk Sool and became the second-highest-ranking Kuk Sool practitioner in the Chicago area. His continual practice and dedication awarded him many grand championship titles throughout the country, including placement in every event at the World Kuk Sool Won Tournament in Korea in 2002. Sa Bum Nym began running a dojang (school) as an assistant instructor in 1991 and began teaching full time a year later. He has now become an instrumental part of the United Martial Science Federation and completed the requirements to become promoted to Chief Instructor of the Midwest Region in October 2006.

In January 2003, Sa Bum Nym created *Art of the Warrior: Martial Arts Magazine*. Sa Bum Nym, with the help and support of many others, has been fortunate to tour the world interviewing, training, and promoting this new martial arts magazine. To date, this independent publication has produced more than 70,000 magazines and has readership all over the world. *Art of the Warrior* has its own design and photography department and has been a great service to countless martial arts schools and organizations since its conception. This magazine's work can be seen in various other media outlets.

Sa Bum Nym has set himself on a road traveled by very few. His martial arts career has been nurtured by many, including, but not limited to, his family, formal instructors, and extended martial arts family. It was these individuals that have played an intricate role in Sa Bum Nym's development over the last 20 years in martial arts. In addition to his three formal instructors, Sa Bum Nym has traveled the world learning from several Grand Masters, Masters, and Instructors such as: Grandmaster In Hyuk Suh, Grandmaster Anthony Muhammad, Grand Master In Sun Seo, Grand Master Al Tracey, Grand Master C.S. Kim, Grand Master Rudy Timmerman, Grand Master Moses Powell, Grand Master Degenerberg, Grand Master John Davis, Grand Master Bill Wallace, Grand Master Bill McCloud, Grand Master Jimmy Jones, Grand Master Shorty Mills, Grand Master Preston Baker, Master Sung Jin Suh, Master Barry Harmon, Master Cheryl Cherowitz, Master Larry Tankson, Master Anthony Price, Master Terry Creamer, and countless other instructors from around the world.